Church Structure That Works

Turning Dysfunction into Health

Written Endorsements

Church Structure That Works is a helpful and practical guide as a local body of believers considers how to do the work of the church. There is much wisdom in this book. You will read it with profit

Daniel L. Akin
President, Southeastern Baptist Theological Seminary

With both a scholar's mind and a pastor's heart, Bill Blanchard expertly fills a huge void in the realm of church structure. His book, *Church Structure That Works,* offers a practical guide to effectively doing the work of the Lord through the local church. I heartily commend this book to anyone faithfully serving the bride of Christ.

James A. Austin
Executive Director, South Carolina Baptist Convention

There has never been a time in my over forty years of ministry that I have read a book or attended a conference about church structure. Most churches have generally accepted the structure of the church as it has been passed from generation to generation.

As a pastor and denominational servant, it has been my experience that many problems within the local church are the result of inappropriate church structure. Often the church is governed by a constitution and bylaws that have been duplicated from other churches with only minor changes or, perhaps, written to address specific problems. Therefore, many churches experience failures and problems only to repeat them because the guiding documents are not scripturally based.

Bill Blanchard's book is long overdue. Through the fervent study of the Scriptures and his experience as a pastor, Bill Blanchard has written a book detailing a biblically principled church structure that will be very helpful to pastors and church leaders everywhere as they strive to organize the church for effective ministry, missions, and evangelism.

Robert A. Boswell
Assistant Executive Director, Georgia Baptist Convention

Like a bad sound system, poor church structure is only noticed when something goes wrong. In *Church Structure That Works,* Dr. Bill Blanchard eliminates the perennial confusion surrounding the "means" and "ends" of building an effective and efficient local church organizational apparatus. Throughout the book, Blanchard reveals his leadership acumen by clearly and masterfully weaving together all of the necessary elements that comprise church structure—including theological commitments, biblical principles, organizational theory and practical application. By doing so, he fills a much-neglected gap in the church leadership-administration literary genre and strikes the delicate balance of providing pastors, professors and lay leaders alike with a timeless, multicultural and cross-cultural tool that serves as a textbook, workbook, handbook and manual, all rolled up in one. *Church Structure That Works* is an invaluable gift to the local church from a man with a professor's mind and a pastor's heart.

Frederick Cardoza II
Associate Dean and Professor, Midwestern Baptist Theological Seminary

In *Church Structure That Works,* Bill Blanchard offers biblical principles and concrete examples that pastors and church leaders can use to re-engineer their church structure for staff empowerment, accountability and efficiency. This book has been very helpful and affirming as our church has reviewed its structure.

Tommy Ferrell
Senior Pastor, Briarlake Baptist Church

I have served as a pastor in the United States, a missionary in Africa, and a supervisor of missionaries in South America, and have been employed as a seminary missions professor for the past four years. I believe that Dr. Blanchard's new book fills a much needed gap in our understanding of ecclesiology and, more importantly, its proper, practical application. Although it is obvious that every international and North American church start begins with some kind of structure, all too often missiologists do not give adequate attention to the practical details of church form and government.

Many church-planting practitioners allow the structure for new church plants to either evolve or be copied from denominational templates. *Church Structure That Works: Turning Dysfunction into Health* examines the issue of church government from a scriptural perspective, applying biblical scholarship to the practical insights of a pastor with 30 years of experience. The result is a congregationalism that balances pastoral authority with competent lay accountability and ministry, allowing the church structure to model the body of Christ, rather than restrict her. Pastors, missionaries, church planters, seminary professors, church leaders and church members will be greatly helped by reading and applying this book.

Robin Hadaway
Former Missionary and Associate Professor of Missions
Midwestern Baptist Theological Seminary

Many churches seem to base their ministry on pragmatism without giving significant thought to whether or not what they are doing is in accordance with the Word or the will of God. Other churches get in a traditional rut and continue to operate the same way they have been operating for years without any real understanding of why they function as they do. Yet other churches are plagued with selfish members who attempt to exercise their power in a destructive way.

In his book, *Church Structure That Works: Turning Dysfunction into Health,* Bill Blanchard has developed a biblical approach to church polity which serves as a model for a properly functioning church. This remarkably helpful book has been born out of the crucible of personal experience and a conscientious study of God's Word. It effectively addresses an area of ecclesiology that has been sorely neglected for years.

Gerald Harris
Editor, *The Christian Index*

When I left for the mission field twenty years ago after nine years in pastoral ministry, I must confess that I harbored a hope and prayer that "it would be different" on the mission field, and that somehow churches there would not suffer some of the all-too-common problems of U.S. churches: long and acrimonious business meetings, pastors suffering from burnout, and power struggles resulting in the firings of capable men of God. Unfortunately, I found that both established churches and new church plants in South America and North Africa—the two fields where I have served as a church planter—suffered these same problems, a result of systemic weaknesses described in *Church Structure That Works: Turning Dysfunction into Health.* Without a doubt, each one of these churches that I encountered in the third world would benefit greatly from Dr. Blanchard's insightful application of biblical principles in the formation and ongoing life and structure of the local church. Whether your context is rural or urban, national or international, I believe that this book will be of great benefit to your ministry.

Rich Hutchens
Career Missionary

Our church had just completed a successful journey to a simpler, more biblical church structure when Bill Blanchard and I first talked about this vital topic almost a decade ago. Now, with the wisdom and insights born of leading two churches through similar transitions, Blanchard offers a wealth of practical, biblical guidance that will help many churches bring clarity and health to an area of church life too often characterized by confusion and conflict. I heartily commend *Church Structure That Works: Turning Dysfunction into Health.*

Tim McCoy
Senior Pastor, Ingleside Baptist Church

Sorrows and heartaches are just a part of life. They are, in the final analysis, unavoidable. Nevertheless, there are "church sorrows and heartaches" that not only could be avoided but *should be* avoided at all costs. I thank God for a pastor like Dr. Bill Blanchard who has identified a root cause for so many difficulties within the church and has known how to address it. This book is essential reading for all pastors, ministerial staff members, church planters, missionaries, deacons, and other church leaders.

Paige Patterson
President, Southwestern Baptist Theological Seminary

On the mission field, church planters passionately seek to develop new believers, leaders and groups that will hopefully become new churches. But when these new disciples become a church, then what? How will the new church function? Thankfully, Bill Blanchard's *Church Structure That Works: Turning Dysfunction into Health* answers this critical question with a simple biblical plan to organize a body of believers, whether an established church or a new work, in any context or culture. I recommend this book without hesitation.

Mike Pineda
Career Missionary

A lot is being written and discussed about church health these days, but the solutions to the problems seem to be elusive as suggestions range between over-spiritualizing the issues and resorting to secular organizational models. Dr. Bill Blanchard provides an encouraging alternative in his book *Church Structure That Works* that is practical and biblical, and comes from successful implementation. Applying this model could move many churches beyond dysfunction to effective ministry, witness and growth.

Jerry Rankin
President, International Mission Board

As a practicing Christian attorney, I am often called upon to offer advice and counsel to churches in turmoil. Having done so for almost 30 years has convinced me that the traditional church structure is in desperate need of revision. *Church Structure That Works: Turning Dysfunction into Health* provides invaluable insight and advice, and the adoption of its principles will no doubt eliminate much of the strife and conflict that unfortunately permeates many churches today.

Hoyt Samples
Attorney

In a day when the church is under attack from seemingly every angle, the need for effective organization has never been greater. Waste, whether it is in time, talent or finances, has never been a part of Christ's desire for His church. In *Church Structure That Works,* Bill Blanchard sets forth biblically-based, Christ-honoring concepts that cut through the clutter that so often typifies congregational organization. Harry

Stonecipher, vice-president of the Boeing Company, once asked his listeners to contrast the difference between a warehouse and a modern airplane. "The warehouse may contain two million parts, but the airplane, to quote an old line, is 'two million parts flying together in close formation.'"

Such could also be the definition of the well-organized church. Bill Blanchard knows congregational organization like Stonecipher knows airplanes, and he understands that Christ's church is built on teamwork between vocational staff and laity. Just how close the formation is between those two groups and whether all the parts can work together in varying moments of stress, depend on teamwork. Bill Blanchard provides a blueprint to pull those vastly different parts out of the warehouse and align them in a way that provides for a highly efficient organization, one that is fine-tuned to make the greatest evangelical impact for the kingdom of Christ.

Joe Westbury
Managing Editor, *The Christian Index*

Church Structure That Works

Turning Dysfuntion into Health

Bill Blanchard

VMI Publishers • Sisters, Oregon

Church Structure That Works

Published by
VMI Publishers
Sisters, Oregon
www.vmipublishers.com

Scripture taken from the *New King James Version.*

ISBN: 1-933204-55-9
ISBN 13: 978-1-933204-55-0
Library of Congress Control Number: 2007941988

Printed in the USA.

Cover design by Joe Bailen

DEDICATED TO THE GRACIOUS AND SUPPORTIVE CONGREGATIONS OF:

GRAND AVENUE BAPTIST CHURCH
Fort Smith, Arkansas 72904

MOUNTAIN PARK FIRST BAPTIST CHURCH
Stone Mountain, Georgia 30087

Table of Contents

Foreword

Sorrows and heartaches are just a part of life. They are, in the final analysis, unavoidable. Nevertheless, there are "church sorrows and heartaches" that not only could be avoided but should be avoided at all costs. My experience as president at three different institutions for the training of ministers, covering a period of thirty-two years, plus serving as pastor of a number of local churches, has taught me well the tragedies of people in the churches. There is scarcely a week that goes by that I am not called by a brokenhearted pastor or an irate church member or in some other way thrust into the midst of dissension within congregations.

Like any observant pastor, Dr. Bill Blanchard, who holds a Ph.D. in Biblical Studies from Southern Baptist Theological Seminary in Louisville, Kentucky, and who has extensive years of service as a senior pastor, has observed these same sorrows and has grown weary of unnecessary church squabbles that occur all over the world. He has worked determinedly across the years to find a biblical way to structure a New Testament church, suggesting a foundation and framework for successfully handling these issues. Though these suggestions do not guarantee growth—only the Holy Spirit can do that—they do encourage it. Out of his scholarly research and pastoral experience, Dr. Blanchard has provided this superb volume entitled *Church Structure That Works: Turning Dysfunction into Health.*

Dr. Blanchard has one of those remarkable personalities that combines the ability to be a strong, decisive leader with ironclad convictions, and yet he does so with the gentleness of a tender shepherd working with his flock. Indeed, some of that remarkable combination of attributes becomes apparent to the reader as he reads this volume and its helpful appendices.

It is a surprising fact that so few books have ever appeared on church structure. Most books about the church either focus primarily on theology or else have become nothing more than manuals describing how certain things were achieved in a given location. There is nothing wrong with either of these. In fact, the present volume is based solidly upon an appropriate ecclesiology or theology of the church. However, it also fills an incomparable need, namely, to provide a book on how you actually go about structuring the local church based on theological moorings that enable that church to plan and produce a significant Christ-honoring congregation, as well as successfully handle conflicts that arise.

Because the principles embodied herein are founded directly upon the Word of God, they can be implemented effectively in just about any size of church, in almost any denomination, and certainly in any culture found in the world. This book moves beyond just theory, and is the result of what has actually been implemented successfully in two congregations, namely, the two to whom this volume is dedicated.

Among the many virtues of this book, there is at least one that I want specifically to mention. Pastors are busy people and, as much as they would like to take time to read long tomes with extensive annotations, it just does not reasonably take place very often. This book is comprehensive but at the same time succinct. One can easily follow the development of the book and quickly ascertain how its suggestions might be implemented in the local congregation.

Church Structure That Works: Turning Dysfunction into Health encourages my mind and heart because I know that if something similar to the structure and plan outlined in this book was inculcated in most of our churches, I would receive far fewer phone calls of desperation than come my way now. I know that Jesus Christ loved the church and gave Himself for her. And, because I love Jesus Christ, I love His church also. When I hear of hurting and sorrowing pastors, I experience a measure of that hurt also. There is quite enough hurt in the world without adding to anybody's burden. I thank God for a pastor like Dr. Bill Blanchard, who has identified a root cause of so many difficulties within the church and has known how to address it. This book is essential reading for all pastors, ministerial staff members, church planters, missionaries, deacons, and other church leaders. May God bless Bill Blanchard and this helpful volume.

Dr. Paige Patterson
President of Southwestern Baptist Theological Seminary • Fort Worth, Texas

About the Author

Bill Blanchard has a multi-cultural upbringing. He was born in India and reared there for the first 14 years of his life. Upon returning to the United States with his parents, he completed his high school years in Chicago, Illinois, and then graduated from the University of Illinois in Champaign-Urbana, with a degree in Marketing. Bill continued his studies at Southern Baptist Theological Seminary in Louisville, Kentucky, earning M.Div. and Ph.D. degrees. He also completed advanced graduate studies at Hebrew Union University in Cincinnati, Ohio. He has served as a senior pastor for 30 years. For eight of those years he took on the additional responsibilities as a trustee of the International Mission Board, the last two years of which he served as its chairman. Bill has been married to Lara since 1976, and they are the parents of three grown children. Bill is the senior pastor of Mountain Park First Baptist Church in suburban Atlanta, Georgia, and is an adjunct professor for New Orleans Baptist Theological Seminary Extension Center (North Georgia campus).

Chapter One

Can You Relate to This?

When my wife and I first began to serve in a church together, we had a passion for the Lord, but were very young, inexperienced, and ill-equipped. The first church where I served as a student pastor didn't even have running water, and my wife was still in her late teens.

After graduating from seminary, when we were called to our first full-time church position, the staff consisted of a volunteer music director in her 60s, a part-time secretary and me. That was it. During our 11 years of service there, the church experienced uninterrupted growth, but about five years into that pastorate we ran into a vicious power struggle that I had never anticipated. I was young and idealistic. All I wanted to do was serve in a church where the truth of the Scriptures could be presented in a relevant way. I wanted to see lives affected for all of eternity by Jesus Christ. The hostility that we experienced, however, almost wrecked our lives.

About half way through that pastorate I was confronted by an extremely influential and self-appointed lay leader who felt that my time of service in that church was over. He met with me privately and let me know in no uncertain terms that it was time for my wife, young children and me to move on. Later, I discovered that he had done the very same thing to my three predecessors! When I didn't accommodate his demands, things got ugly, and I must admit that my courage wavered for about a week. We knew that the Lord did not redeem humanity to function in such disarray.

It was during this time of insecurity that I called my elderly, widowed mother and asked her if my wife, three children and I could move into her basement if I were fired. Unfortunately, many pastors are, and have been, faced with this type of humiliation—and for no good reason. My wife and I prayed through this ordeal and resolved that the Lord wanted us to remain faithful and strong. During this time of turmoil, we never attempted to move to another church by distributing my résumé to those within our circles of influence. We stayed where we were, faced the challenges head-on, led the church through that conflict, and it was only then that that little church began to grow well.

Are you able to relate to this struggle? If the Lord called you into His service and you believed with all of your heart and mind and soul that He wanted you to make a real difference for Him for the few short years of your life here, did the fruit of a poor church structure almost wreck your future? Have you ever come to the end of your ministerial rope in a local church setting? That's about the time you ask, "God, isn't there a better way to accomplish Your mission in the local church?"

It was out of this quandary that I began to search for answers. I was amazed to discover that there was almost nothing in print relevant to this matter. So many denominational leaders claim that their brand of Christianity is based upon the complete trustworthiness of the Scriptures, and yet there is almost nothing in print to help us structure our churches based upon a biblical model. I was also surprised to learn that very few other pastors have ever studied biblical church structure carefully. Yes, I know that a book on church structure may not be the attention-grabbing topic of the day, but if you can relate to what I've just described, then this may be one of the most pivotal books you'll ever read.

Now, back to the story. This difficult time became a defining moment for me. It motivated me to become well-acquainted with biblical church structure, and our church began to move in that direction. Just as we were getting ready to make that transition, we felt the Lord calling me to become the senior pastor of the Grand Avenue Baptist Church in Fort Smith, Arkansas. This church had a distinguished past, but unfortunately it had recently been caught up in a series of conflicts. Their most recent crisis had made them very ready for a different church structure. I didn't have all the answers, but I was well on the way to developing a model that was biblical and effective. Fortunately, this church was filled with many competent, godly, supportive, intelligent people who helped take something good and make it even better.[1] Fifteen months after arriving there, Grand Avenue had a new constitution and bylaws under which the congregation operated very well and efficiently. With those issues settled, we were able to focus on the real mission of the church.

After seven wonderful years in Fort Smith, a gentleman whom we had never met or even talked to on the phone[2] got my résumé from a third party and placed it into the hands of the Pastor Search Committee of Mountain Park First Baptist Church in suburban Atlanta, Georgia. In April of 2005, we began our ministry in this new setting.

Reviewing their constitution and bylaws wasn't the first thing on my radar, but the church leadership told me they knew it needed revising. They were simply waiting for a new senior pastor before tackling such an important project. I soon discovered that their constitution and bylaws were written and treated as one document! On several levels, it truly did need to be redone.

The church elected a task force[3] to draw up a biblical church structure. This group of men and women, with a wide range of backgrounds, interests and professional expertise worked tirelessly with our ministerial staff to make sure all the bases were covered in a God-honoring way. They produced superb documents, and the congregation approved them. If only the constitution and bylaws had always been that way!

There were huge challenges and a lot of personal pain during our early days there. But there were also a lot of godly men and women who had vision and who worked very hard to move forward in building an even better church. It felt good to know that the structure on which we were now building was more biblically sound than ever before.

Although we hate to admit it, many of our churches are in a mess relationally and organizationally. Examples are so varied, but the messes are typically caused by selfishness—some want their pet project promoted and others want their own plans adopted. Still others who have a personal agenda want to undermine leadership or are concerned with issues of authority.

We all see the reports. They come out almost every year. The firings of pastors are at or near record levels. Have you ever noticed that one of the top "reasons" for these dismissals has to do with who is in charge (the issue of authority)? Both pastors and lay church leaders have seen the dysfunction, felt it, heard of it, experienced it, and even smelled it to the point of becoming sickened by it.

The grief and pain from this dysfunction have caused many church leaders to just want to give up and walk away in search of something better. This tragic reality is especially embarrassing to admit to our detractors and to those who are far from God. At the same time, there's something about our churches that I love and can't stop loving, and that something is actually Someone, Jesus Christ, who gave His own life for the church that He might present her one day as the perfectly adorned bride of Christ.

I need to mention something very important, however: *A proper church structure does not ensure spiritual or numerical growth; all it does is facilitate growth. It's only the Holy Spirit who can bring people to a relationship with Jesus Christ.* But when people experience that relationship with Jesus Christ and come together in local congregations for worship, fellowship, discipleship, ministry and outreach, it can be magnetic if it's "done decently and in order" (1 Corinthians 14:40).

I wish when I was younger that I'd known how to do this properly for effective ministry and growth. Such information wasn't available then, and there's still a paucity of books on hand dealing with this subject. Pastors and church leaders, *I believe that one of the biggest heartaches you and I face is fighting a non-biblical church structure that will not allow us to accomplish what God has called us to do.*

These challenges lead to low morale and discouraged leadership among our ranks. The fruit of improper church structure can drain your enthusiasm and kill your vision faster than almost anything else. You need hope that something can be done about the dysfunction around you; this book may be the tool you so desperately need to turn that dysfunction into health. If you're a missionary or church planter who has the privilege of building a church from scratch, then this book may be the tool you need to do it correctly right from the beginning.

1. There was one particular lay person from the Grand Avenue Baptist Church, Mr. Jeff Roberts, who needs to be especially acknowledged at this point. Jeff was passionate about biblical church structure too. He also brought a keen business perspective and an analytical mind to this project. Our deep trust for and friendship with one another allowed us to challenge each other, knowing that our ultimate objective was to produce a constitution and bylaws that would be biblically accurate and practical. My friendship with him remains deep and life-long, and I believe that the Lord has used Jeff's input in this project in ways that will enhance His Kingdom significantly well into the future.

2. Rev. John Ashby was the point of contact. He was 79 years old at the time. At this time, we didn't know that this church in Atlanta even existed or that they were without a senior pastor. We declined their overtures for almost a year before the Lord really got our attention.

3. The 19 laypersons who served on this task force are as follows (alphabetically): Phillip Brenner, Eric Brown, Ginger Brown, Jackie Brugh (vice-chairperson), Vicki Buice, Lisa Cohorst, Gordon Davidson (chairman), Rick Deemer, Chris Garrett (secretary), Marc Gentry, Keith Hill, Bruce Miller, Doris Miller, Wayne Patterson, Angela Shelton, Rhonda Williams, Steve Wilson, Lamar Worthy, and Marvin Wyatt. Aside from me, the eight other vocational ministers who served on this task force are as follows (alphabetically): Will Blanchard, Bob Bochat, Debbie Braswell, Jerry Counselman, Doug Cox, Michael Deese, Mike Holt, and Richard King. Of these vocational ministers, Doug Cox was serving as the Executive Pastor of the MPFBC at the time. He and I were complete strangers before our arrival at the MPFBC, but he soon became not only a colleague but also one of my most trusted friends. All of the members of this task force leaned upon him heavily throughout this entire project as he bore most of the grunt work, and his contribution to this manuscript has been extremely valuable. I also owe a very special debt of gratitude to one of my sisters, Carol Hackler, who later helped me express the truths in this book more effectively with her excellent journalistic skills.

Chapter Two

Why Is It Like This?

Many of you can probably relate to the difficulties I've just described, either because you've been there or you've seen it from a distance. A possible root cause for this dysfunction could be the way that most churches are organized, the way they're structured, the way their constitution and bylaws are drafted.

Perhaps it would be helpful at the outset to define several important terms. *The articles of incorporation,* usually no longer than one page, are *the constitution.* This document calls the entity into legal existence in the state where the church is located.

The bylaws then explain how the legal entity will be governed. Amazingly, and unfortunately, in some churches these two distinctively different documents are written and treated as one. The governing of the entity under its bylaws must always be within the framework and purposes set out in its articles (constitution), and the bylaws may neither nullify nor supersede the articles.[1] Revisions to the bylaws are common; revisions to a constitution are rare.

As you may know, a church's constitution and bylaws are the key instruments that determine how a church functions. They are the governing documents of a church. Unfortunately, the majority of churches have formulated their constitution and bylaws simply by modifying what they've seen in use elsewhere. They went down the street to neighboring churches for samples of their constitution and bylaws, tweaked them a bit, and put them in place in their own church. They've given these critical instruments very little biblical scrutiny simply because they didn't know what to look for. But we can't blame them too much. They haven't done anything wrong intentionally. The leaders just didn't know what else to do. In fact, relatively few pastors and professors have ever carefully studied biblical church structure, so there's very little information to guide them or for them to share. It's a surprising fact that so few books and almost no reputable publications on church structure have ever been published.

Here's something else to think about. Why is it that over 90% of all churches in this country and throughout the world never grow beyond three hundred in attendance? Consider this. What do the following words and phrases have in common: elections, voting, board meetings, parliamentary procedures, committees, and majority rule? None of these words or phrases is in the Bible, at least not in a favorable light. It would seem, therefore, that what we've done for the most part, at least in the United States of America, is take the American notion of a democratic voting process and impose it on the church. And, as a result, our churches are often about as effective as our state and federal governments, both of which are often paralyzed by bureaucratic gridlock! All of this bureaucracy can hinder a local congregation's growth. We're so busy maintaining ourselves that we don't have the energy to reach out and grow. Yes, there is a dilemma. We haven't known much about biblical church structure or known how freeing and healthy it can be.

Consequently, pastors and churches suffer through difficulty after difficulty. When problems surface, there's no clear channel for resolving them. The leadership becomes swamped by trying to do too much of the work themselves while the average member becomes a bystander. Authority issues surface. The local congregation functions at less than prime. There's no instrument to help them function in a healthy, biblical way, and no biblical guide for working through these problems. Doesn't this help explain the quagmire in which many churches find themselves?

The information in this book will help you build an effective church structure. It's a biblical model of delegating authority with responsibility to spiritually mature and competent Christians, yet it includes an adequate system of checks and balances based upon principles from God's Word.

1. See David Barton, *Original Intent: The Courts, the Constitution, and Religion,* Aledo, Texas, WallBuilder Press, Fourth edition, 2005, p. 247.

Chapter Three

What Will Guide Us?

It's intriguing to note that the writers of the New Testament didn't provide a clear and explicit pattern for one and only one system of church structure. This helps to explain why, over the years, several different kinds of organizational models have emerged among Christian denominations. These various forms of church governance are simply a mingling of biblical principles, coupled with local dynamics, and merged with cultural and historical considerations.

In the sovereign plan of God, however, it could be that this lack of precise biblical instruction was actually intentional for two reasons. First, it may have been God's way of saying that His church should not be tied structurally to any one particular culture. For example, if there had been a specific organizational model for the first century church in Jerusalem, it probably wouldn't be transferable point-for-point to every culture all over the world more than two thousand years later.

A second reason why God may have left this somewhat vague in the Scriptures is that you and I need to build our respective structures partly around the unique gifts and talents in our individual churches. That is, we're to be organized around what we have (the giftedness of our respective members), rather than what we don't have.

With this in mind, modern-day church governance will usually fall into one of the following five broad camps[1]:

- Presbyterian
- Episcopalian (Roman Catholic, Orthodox, Anglican, Methodist)
- Congregational (Baptists, Congregationalists, some Lutherans)
- Erastian (national state churches)
- Minimalist or non-governmental (Quakers)

With this as our context, there are four broad principles that will guide this study:

- **Principle One**—In the ultimate sense, the local church is to be governed by the Lord Jesus Christ as revealed in the Scriptures.
- **Principle Two**—It's presupposed that the Scriptures are completely trustworthy in every area. Therefore, nothing within the Scriptures will be disregarded or explained away for the sake of expediency.
- **Principle Three**—Although there is authority and seniority within the body of Christ, there is no such thing as the superiority of one Christian over another. All believers have equal access to God without the need for an intermediary.
- **Principle Four**—While it's true that the church is a *divine* institution where proper biblical theology is essential, it's also a *legal* institution that must comply with the laws of the state, to the extent possible. There are and have been those rare occasions when it is impossible for Christ followers to comply with all the laws of the land because the laws are atheistic and corrupt. In such instances, the Scriptures are replete with illustrations in which a type of civil disobedience is preferred, and the church must go underground.

  A more common legal scenario, however, is when a court must redefine the structure of a church if that church is not in compliance with the corporate laws of the state. This may occur when a church without a good constitution and bylaws is dissolved and the steps in the church's documents are not in compliance with that state's corporate laws.

  Another example would relate to a church certifying the tax-free contributions of its members. Since a church enjoys certain tax benefits as a nonprofit corporation, it must comply with nonprofit corporate legal requirements, which includes filing for tax-exempt status with the Internal Revenue Service. Unfortunately, many people do not discover the need to comply with these legal requirements until their church is hit with an ugly lawsuit. (Note: I cannot stress enough the importance of having both a lawyer and an accountant involved in the process of writing the constitution and bylaws and filing them with the appropriate agencies. This is not a do-it-yourself project! See chapter 10 for further information in this regard.)

Finally, a church must recognize that it is not only a *divine* institution with *legal* obligations, but it must consider the *human/relational* elements among its membership as well.

It is my intention that these four guiding principles help all of us develop and implement a structure in local churches throughout the world that is "honorable…, not only in the sight of the Lord, but also in the sight of men" (2 Corinthians 8:21).

1. For a defense of these views by their respective proponents, please consult *Perspectives on Church Government: Five Views of Church Polity,* edited by Chad Owen Brown and R. Stanton Norman, Broadman and Holman Publishers, 2004.

CHAPTER FOUR

THE SOLUTION

There is ample evidence in the New Testament to show that the words *elder/presbyter, pastor/shepherd,* and *bishop/overseer* refer to the same person or church office. In his famous commentary on Philippians, J.B. Lightfoot, a well-known scholar from a former era, states, "It is a fact now generally recognized by theologians of all shades of opinion, that in the language of the New Testament the same officer in the Church is called indifferently 'bishop' (επισκοπος) and 'elder' or 'presbyter' (πρεσβυτερος)."[1]

The first of these words, "elder," can also be translated "presbyter," and from it we get the word Presbyterian. It's a transliteration of the Greek word πρεσβυτερος. Elder does not necessarily refer to a person's age, although age and experience can apply, but primarily the term applies to one's spiritual maturity. For example, Timothy was the elder of the church in Ephesus although he was actually a very young man. It is a given that elders must model godly living and teach God's Word correctly, but there's another important way for them to inspire maturity in Christ followers. It's by encouraging others to become involved *in* ministry rather than be just spectators *of* ministry. Mature Christians will naturally want to bring others alongside themselves, helping them find their unique niche for service in the body of Christ. In fact, one evidence of maturity is a willingness to take on responsibility.

The second word, "pastor," comes from the Greek verb ποιμαινω, which means to provide pastoral care by feeding and nourishing others from God's Word. This biblical imagery is of a shepherd tending his sheep by caring for them, defending them against intruders, knowing them by name, numbering them, and protecting them in the folds.

The third word, "bishop," comes from the Greek word **επισκοπος**,[2] which is defined as a church leader who oversees the management and governance of the church. It's from this Greek word that we get the English word Episcopalian. That particular denomination refers to its leaders as bishops, a word that is seen in several translations of the Bible.

Interestingly enough, elders (Titus 1:5–9), pastors (Ephesians 4:11–12), and bishops (1 Tim. 3:2) are all responsible for accurately teaching God's Word.

The key point is to understand that all of the words above are addressed to the same church leader. For instance, in 1 Peter 5:1–5, the great apostle was essentially saying "to the elders/presbyters, be good pastors/shepherds as you lead/ manage/govern/offer direction to the congregation as bishops/overseers." The same thing is true of Acts 20:17 and 28, where the apostle Paul exhorted the "*elders* of the church" at Ephesus to serve as *overseers* over "all the flock…to *shepherd* the church of God which He purchased with His own blood." So, it doesn't really matter what you call this individual; these titles simply refer to three different tasks expected of the same person or church office. With this in mind, God has called some to full-time ministry. Although these individuals may be called by a variety of titles and descriptions, I prefer to call these vocational servant leaders "pastors," and in our church they form our Pastoral Leadership Team (PLT).[3] They are all called to function as elders/presbyters, pastors/shepherds, and bishops/overseers.

It would be impossible for these vocational servant leaders to do all the work of mentoring, recruiting, providing pastoral care and governing the church. They'd either wear out or become bottlenecks for ministry. For these obvious reasons, they need to delegate some of their responsibilities to vital lay leadership groups.

Although these lay groups may be given a variety of titles and names, I would suggest the following:

1. **EQUIPPING MINISTRY TEAM.**[4] This group of lay leaders seeks to fulfill the function of **elders/presbyters** as they assist others in developing spiritual maturity. How? Through helping church members become involved in various ministry teams according to their SHAPE.[5]

   Obviously, spiritual maturity is achieved in a variety of ways, but, assuming there are no concerns with health issues or unusual family responsibilities, ministry involvement is crucial in the development of one's spiritual maturity. Following Christ is not simply a matter of devotion to prayer and mental assent to important doctrinal matters. Rather, it is primarily a spiritual relationship whereby the Holy Spirit of God is allowed to flow through Christ followers in ministry to others.

2. DEACON MINISTRY TEAM. This lay leadership group fulfills the function of **pastors/shepherds** through various aspects of pastoral care such as feeding, nourishing, caring, counseling, seeking those far from God, etc. Later in this book, a model will be proposed in which deacons function as spiritual mentors, not just spiritual managers, thus including many other members within the church in lay pastoral care ministry.
3. MANAGEMENT TEAM.[6] These lay leaders fulfill the function of **bishops/overseers** by exercising oversight in the management and governance of the church. This would include administrating, directing, guiding and leading the business affairs of the church.

For simply practical reasons a fourth lay leadership group, the Nominating Committee, is needed within the church. While there is not any specific biblical precedent for this group, it is needed to select persons to serve in the other lay leadership groups. The rationale for this entity is provided near the end of the following chapter. (It is the need for an ongoing selection process after the era of the apostles when leaders were appointed.) The purpose of the Nominating Committee is to identify those lay leaders who may have the leadership skills as well as the proper SHAPE profile for a specific ministry.

I refer to these vital lay leadership groups as The Big Four. All of them, with crucial input from the PLT, are to serve together as a unified whole—not competitively, but cooperatively—in developing people into fully devoted Christ followers.

Do you think you've grasped these important insights? Can you see that *a proper and effective biblical church structure will include:*

1. A lay leadership group who will help others mature spiritually by getting them vitally involved in ministry.
2. Another lay leadership group who is responsible for pastoral care.
3. Another lay leadership group who is responsible for managing and governing the church.
4. A Nominating Committee who nominates members for the above groups.

The great beauty of this structure is that it is not only biblically principled, it is also very effective and can work in any size of church, in any denomination, and in any area or culture of the world. Why? Because, although nomenclature may vary, this arrangement is based upon the thrust of the eternal values and doctrines found in the Scriptures. Even if you are serving as the one and only bi-vocational minister of a very small group of Christ followers in a storefront setting, or in a house-church environment, or even in an underground "non-registered" church, this structure can still work. You, as the one and only elder/pastor/bishop, should extend yourself through others—no matter how few in number they might be—in these four areas, even if you can find only one or two people to serve as members of each group. You might be few in number, especially at the start, but you can still have your own Big Four!

With this church structure in mind, in the immediately following pages you're invited to study the constitution and bylaws of the Mountain Park First Baptist Church. They are biblical, refreshing, legal, and even easy to read! Because it's also the linchpin to the biblical structure explained in this book, you would do well to read it before reading the next chapter.

1. *St. Paul's Epistle to the Philippians,* J.B. Lightfoot, 1868; revised, 1953, Zondervan Publishing House, Grand Rapids, Michigan, p. 95.
2. Literally, this word means "one who over (επι) sees (σκοπος)."
3. Please consult Appendix #6 throughout the course of your reading of this book in order to be reminded of the meaning of this acronym, as well as several others.
4. Normally, I prefer the phrase "ministry team" to the word "committee" for two reasons. First, the word "ministry" is a good biblical word. Second, the word "team" conveys the fact that all of the members are working for the same cause and pulling in the same direction. On the other hand, if you prefer the word "committee," that is perfectly acceptable so long as the committee functions as a ministry team. Regardless, please don't let nomenclature be the issue.
5. SHAPE is an acronym, first mentioned by Rick Warren in *The Purpose Driven Church,* that stands for **S**piritual Gifts, **H**eart/Passion, **A**bilities, **P**ersonality, and **E**xperiences. See Appendix #3 for details.
6. This team can be called by a variety of other names such as Administrative Leadership Team (ALT), Strategic Leadership Team (SLT), Board of Overseers, or Board of Directors.

OUR VISION IS TO DEVELOP PEOPLE
INTO FULLY DEVOTED FOLLOWERS OF JESUS CHRIST

CONSTITUTION AND BYLAWS

Approved by vote of the Church on May 21, 2006

MOUNTAIN PARK
FIRST BAPTIST CHURCH
5485 Five Forks Trickum Rd
Stone Mountain, Georgia 30087

Dr. Bill Blanchard, Senior Pastor

TABLE OF CONTENTS

CONSTITUTION

BYLAWS

CONSTITUTION

PREAMBLE

We adopt, declare, and establish this Constitution for the purpose of preserving and securing the principles of our faith, and to the end that this body of believers may be governed in an orderly manner consistent with the teachings of Holy Scripture.

ARTICLE I — Name

This body of believers shall be known as Mountain Park First Baptist Church, Inc., of Stone Mountain, Georgia (referred to as the "Church").

ARTICLE II — Purpose

Desiring to glorify God the Father through His unique Son, Jesus Christ, the Head of the Church, in the power of the Holy Spirit, and affirming the five eternal purposes of worship/magnification, evangelism/missions, fellowship/membership, discipleship/maturity, and service/ministry, the purposes of Mountain Park First Baptist Church are to magnify God, bring people to Jesus, call believers to membership, develop members in spiritual maturity, and equip them for ministry.

ARTICLE III — STATEMENT OF FAITH

We believe that the sixty-six books of the Bible were written by men divinely inspired by God, are completely trustworthy, and are the basis for our beliefs. This Church accepts "The Baptist Faith and Message" (2000 edition), which is incorporated herein by reference and made a part hereof, as an affirmation of our basic Christian beliefs and as a general statement of our faith.

ARTICLE IV — Church Government and Affiliations

Under the Lordship of Jesus Christ, the membership retains the exclusive right of self-government of this Church. This Church is not subject to control by any other ecclesiastical body, but recognizes the obligations of Southern Baptist churches to carry out ministries for the extension of Christ's Kingdom. While maintaining its autonomy, the Church will, as the members of the Church determine, cooperate with and support the Gwinnett Metro Baptist Association, the Georgia Baptist Convention, and the Southern Baptist Convention so long as these entities continue to adhere to "The Baptist Faith and Message" (2000 edition).

ARTICLE V — Adoption and Amendments

Section 1. This Constitution shall be adopted by a two-thirds ($^2/_3$) affirmative vote of the members present and voting at the church business conference in which it is submitted for adoption.[1]

Section 2. This Constitution may be amended by a two-thirds ($^2/_3$) affirmative vote of those members present and voting at any regular or called Church business conference. Notice of such amendment shall be given through distribution of written material to the members in attendance at Sunday services at least two consecutive Sundays in advance of the Church business conference in which the amendment is to be considered.

BYLAWS

SECTION I — Church Membership

A. General

1. The members of the Church shall consist of all persons who have met the requirements for membership and are listed on the Church membership roll.
2. Mountain Park First Baptist Church, Inc. does not have corporate members as the term "member" is defined in O.C.G.A. Section 14-3-140(22). Church membership does not constitute being a member of the corporate entity known as Mountain Park First Baptist Church, Inc., as that term is defined in O.C.G.A. Section 14-3-140(22). The right of a Mountain Park First Baptist Church, Inc. Church member to vote on the election of the Management Team does not constitute being a "member" of Mountain Park First Baptist Church, Inc. as the term "member" is defined in O.C.G.A. Section 14-3-140(22).

B. Requirements for Church Membership

The requirements for Church membership are as follows:

1. A personal profession of faith in Jesus Christ as Lord and Savior;
2. Baptism by immersion as a believer as a symbol of salvation; and,
3. Completion of the Church Membership Orientation and affirmation of the Church Membership Covenant. Exceptions may occasionally be made when someone's physical condition does not allow them to sit for these extended sessions.

C. Responsibilities of Church Membership

The responsibilities of membership are described in the Church Membership Covenant ("Life Together at Mountain Park") set forth below:

"Life Together at Mountain Park"

We, the members of Mountain Park First Baptist Church, affirm that to be a member of the Mountain Park First Baptist family of faith is to be committed to developing a growing relationship with the Lord Jesus Christ and growing relationships with other members of the Church. In the context of these relationships, we commit to God and to one another that we will earnestly endeavor to do the following under the leadership of the Holy Spirit (all Scriptures are from the *New International Version* unless noted):

1. We will prize and protect the unity of our Church family by:
   a. Acting in love toward other members.
      (1) "Let us therefore make every effort to do what leads to peace and to mutual edification." Romans 14:19
      (2) "Be completely humble and gentle; be patient, bearing with one another in love. Make every effort to keep the unity of the Spirit through the bond of peace." Ephesians 4:2-3
      (3) "Now that you have purified yourselves by obeying the truth so that you have sincere love for your brothers, love one another deeply, from the heart." I Peter 1:22
      (4) "Be kind and compassionate to one another, forgiving each other, just as in Christ God forgave you." Ephesians 4:32
   b. Refusing to gossip and stir up dissension.
      (1) "Do not let any unwholesome talk come out of your mouths, but only what is helpful for building others up according to their needs, that it may benefit those who listen." Ephesians 4:29
      (2) "There are six things the Lord hates…a man who stirs up dissension among brothers." Proverbs 6:16, 19
      (3) "A perverse man stirs up dissension, and a gossip separates close friends." Proverbs 16:28
   c. Honoring and following the leaders.
      (1) "The elders who direct the affairs of the church well are worthy of double honor, especially those whose work is preaching and teaching." I Timothy 5:17
      (2) "Obey your leaders and submit to their authority. They keep watch over you as men who must give an account. Obey them so that their

work will be a joy, not a burden, for that would be of no advantage to you." Hebrews 13:17

d. Resolving conflicts through the scriptural, disciplinary guidelines of our Church.
   (1) "If your brother sins against you, go and show him his fault, just between the two of you. If he listens to you, you have won your brother over. But if he will not listen, take one or two others along, so that 'every matter may be established by the testimony of two or three witnesses.' If he refuses to listen to them, tell it to the church; and if he refuses to listen even to the church, treat him as you would a pagan or a tax collector." Matthew18:15-17
   (2) "...if another Christian is overcome by some sin, you who are godly should gently and humbly help that person back onto the right path. And be careful not to fall into the same temptation yourself." Galatians 6:1 (NLT)

2. We will participate in the ministry of our Church family by:
   a. Attending faithfully and giving regularly.
      (1) "Let us not give up meeting together...but let us encourage one another." Heb. 10:25
      (2) "Every Sunday each of you must put aside some money, in proportion to what you have earned, and save it up."
      I Corinthians 16:2 (TEV)
   b. Discovering our gifts and talents.
      (1) "Serve one another with the particular gifts God has given each of you." I Peter 4:10 (Phillips)
      (2) "It was [God] Who gave some...to be pastors and teachers, to prepare God's people for works of service, so that the body of Christ may be built up." Ephesians 4:11-12
   c. Being equipped to serve.
      "Each of you should look not only to your own interests, but also to the interests of others. Your attitude should be the same as that of Christ Jesus; Who...[took on] the very nature of a servant." Philippians 2:4-7
   d. Developing a servant's heart.
      (1) "But among you it should be quite different. Whoever wants to be a

leader among you must be your servant, and whoever wants to be first must become your slave. For even I, the Son of Man, came here not to be served but to serve others, and to give My life as a ransom for many." Matthew 20:26-28 (NLT)

(2) "You, my brothers, were called to be free. But do not use your freedom to indulge in the sinful nature; rather, serve one another in love." Galatians 5:13

3. We will be a partner in the mission of our Church family by:
   a. Praying for its health and growth.
      (1) "In all my prayers for all of you, I always pray with joy because of your partnership in the gospel." Philippians 1:4-5
      (2) "We have not stopped praying for you and asking God...that you may live a life worthy of the Lord and may please Him in every way; bearing fruit in every good work, growing in the knowledge of God." Colossians 1:9-10
   b. Inviting the unchurched to attend.
      "Then the master told his servant, 'Go out to the roads and country lanes and make them come in, so that My house will be full.'" Luke 14:23
   c. Warmly welcoming those who visit.
      "So, warmly welcome each other into the church, just as Christ has warmly welcomed you; then God will be glorified."
      Romans 15:7 (Living Bible)
   d. Sharing Christ as we have opportunity both here and around the world.
      "Always be prepared to give an answer to everyone who asks you to give the reason for the hope that you have." I Peter 3:15

D. Voting Rights of Church Membership

Every member of the Church present in person at a Church business conference shall have the right to vote on all matters presented to the Church for consideration at such Church business conference. Each member of the Church is entitled to one vote. Voting by proxy or absentee ballot is prohibited.

E. Termination of Church Membership

A member shall be removed from the Church membership roll and his or her Church membership terminated for any one of the following reasons:

(1) Death;

(2) Transfer of membership to another church; and when the Church office is informed that a member has joined another church, and that church does not notify the Church to delete such person from the Church membership roll, the Church office will contact the other church for verification, and adjust the Church membership roll accordingly;

(3) Personal written request by the member; or,

(4) Exclusion by the action of the Church when the member's life and conduct are inconsistent with the Scriptures in such a way that the member hinders the ministry influence of the Church. All matters of church discipline, including exclusion, shall be guided by a concern for redemption, reformation, and reconciliation rather than punishment, and shall be first handled by the Management Team in the spirit of Matthew 18:15-17, before any presentation by the Management Team, only, to the Church. If the Management Team determines that church discipline of any member of the Church is appropriate, the Management Team, only, may present to the Church a motion for church discipline of a member of the Church during a Church business conference. Any church discipline of a member of the Church shall require a two-thirds (2/3) affirmative vote of the members present and voting in favor of such motion for church discipline. In every case the person who is the subject of such motion for church discipline shall have the privilege to address the Management Team at a meeting at which the member's church discipline is considered.

F. Restoration of Church Membership

Upon evidence of the excluded person's repentance and reformation, such person excluded by action of the Church shall be restored by a two-thirds (2/3) affirmative vote of the members present and voting for such motion during a Church business conference, upon the recommendation of the Management Team in the spirit of II Corinthians 2:5-11.

SECTION II — Church Business Conferences

A. **Place**

Church business conferences shall be held at 5485 Five Forks Trickum Road, Stone Mountain, Georgia, or such other place as may be designated by the Management Team.

B. **Scheduled Church Business Conferences**

The scheduled business conferences of the Church shall be held quarterly, on a Sunday night, with the annual Church business conference being in October.

C. **Called Church Business Conferences**

The Senior Pastor or the Management Team shall have the authority to call the Church to conference for business whenever it is deemed expedient.

D. **Notice Requirements**

Notice of scheduled and called Church business conferences shall be provided to members two consecutive Sunday mornings prior to the Church business conference. Notice shall include a general description of any business to be transacted and may be given by distribution of written material to the members in attendance at Sunday services, and/or by a verbal announcement to the congregation in attendance at Sunday services.

E. **Procedures**

1. In conducting all Church business conferences, the Church shall be guided by *Robert's Rules of Order*, current edition, except in cases otherwise specifically provided for in the Constitution and Bylaws. A person may be designated by the Chairman of the Management Team to serve as Parliamentarian.
2. The Chairman of the Management Team shall serve as the moderator of all Church business conferences. In the absence of the Chairman of the Management Team, the Vice Chairman of the Management Team shall serve as moderator. In the absence of both, the Executive Pastor shall serve as moderator. In the absence of the three, the Chairman of the Management Team shall designate the moderator.
3. All matters requiring Church approval shall be brought to the attention of

the Management Team at least thirty calendar days before being placed on the agenda of a Church business conference.

4. The Chairman of the Management Team shall establish the agenda for each Church business conference.

F. Quorum

Except as otherwise specifically provided in Section II.G. below, those members entitled to vote and present and voting at a Church business conference duly noticed and called shall constitute a quorum of the membership for the transaction of business.

G. Change in Affiliations; Dissolutions and Mergers

1. All matters relating to any proposal or plan: (a) for affiliation with another church, convention, or association of churches other than Southern Baptist churches; and/or, (b) for dissolution of the Church and/or for disposition of real and personal property and other assets of the Church upon dissolution of the Church; and/or, (c) for merger of the Church with another church or entity; and/or, (d) to alter the corporate character of the Church, shall be referred to and handled by the Management Team, only, before a recommendation by the Management Team to the Church members entitled to vote thereon. The Management Team, only, may recommend a proposal or plan: (a) for affiliation with another church, convention, or association of churches other than Southern Baptist churches; and/or, (b) for dissolution of the Church and/or for disposition of real and personal property and other assets of the Church upon dissolution of the Church; and/or, (c) for merger of the Church with another church or entity; and/or, (d) to alter the corporate character of the Church, to the Church members entitled to vote thereon during any Church business conference. If the Management Team recommends such a proposal or plan, a quorum of not less than fifty-five percent (55%) of the Church members entitled to vote thereon shall be required, and a two-thirds ($^2/_3$) affirmative vote of the Church members entitled to vote and present and voting shall be required to approve and adopt such proposal or plan. For purposes of this Section II.G.1., the Church members entitled to vote on any such proposal or plan shall be only those Church members

who, according to the financial records of the Church, have made a financial contribution to the Church within the twenty-four (24) calendar months immediately preceding the date of the vote of the Management Team to recommend the proposal or plan to the Church members entitled to vote thereon.

2. In the event of the dissolution of the Church, all real and personal property and other assets of the Church shall be distributed in accordance with applicable law.

SECTION III — Church Officers and Staff

A. General

1. The Church is a Georgia nonprofit tax-exempt corporation known as Mountain Park First Baptist Church, Inc.[2] In accordance with the Georgia Non-Profit Corporation Code, the Church must designate individuals to serve in the corporate roles of Directors and Officers.

2. The Management Team shall be the Board of Directors of the Church. The Officers of the Management Team shall be elected by the Management Team and shall be the Officers of the Church. The same individual may not hold more than one Officer position of the Church.[3]

3. The Chairman of the Management Team shall be President of the Church. The Vice Chairman of the Management Team shall be the Vice President of the Church. The Treasurer of the Management Team shall be the Chief Financial Officer of the Church. The Secretary of the Management Team shall be the Secretary of the Church.

4. The President, Vice President, and Chief Financial Officer of the Church are authorized to execute and deliver agreements, contracts, deeds, evidences of indebtedness, and other legal documents on behalf of and binding to the Church, provided that all such agreements, contracts, deeds, evidences of indebtedness, and other legal documents shall be signed by not less than two such Officers.

5. The Secretary shall record and maintain the minutes and records of all Management Team meetings and all Church business conferences, and the Secretary shall, upon request, authenticate all such minutes and Church records.

B. Management Team

1. Qualifications and Responsibilities

The Management Team shall include men and women who are members of the Church, exemplary in their conduct, discreet in judgment, of honest report, full of faith, and conscious that they shall set worthy examples of cooperation, love, and loyalty for all members of the Church.

The principal responsibilities of the Management Team shall be to provide accountability for the Senior Pastor, ensure the financial integrity of the Church, develop and adopt policies relating to the operation of the Church, supervise personnel matters of the Church, and, as the Board of Directors, handle all corporate affairs and business matters involving the Church. These responsibilities shall be administered through the Finance subcommittee, Policy and Legal Issues subcommittee, and Personnel subcommittee, each comprised of approximately one-third ($^1/_3$) of the Management Team members. The members and Chairman of each subcommittee shall be appointed jointly by the Chairman of the Management Team and the Senior Pastor.

a. Senior Pastor Accountability

(1) The Management Team shall provide advice and counsel to the Senior Pastor in the planning, budgeting, staffing, coordination, and implementation functions of the various ministries of the Church.

(2) The Management Team shall evaluate annually the overall performance of the Senior Pastor in the context of his job description.

(3) The Management Team, only, shall make a recommendation to the Church, if necessary, regarding the tenure or dismissal of the Senior Pastor. The Church will not act on any matter relating to the tenure or dismissal of the Senior Pastor without affording the Management Team at

least thirty calendar days to study the matter and make a recommendation to the Church.

b. Financial Integrity
The Management Team shall develop and recommend the annual budget to the Church and shall be responsible for maintaining the integrity of all the financial activities of the Church. Specific financial duties of the Management Team are noted in Section VI.

c. Policy and Legal Issues
(1) The Management Team shall develop and adopt such policies and procedures as are necessary for the effective and orderly functioning of the Church.
(2) The Management Team shall be responsible for handling all legal issues of the Church.

d. Personnel Matters
(1) The Management Team shall update and maintain the Personnel Policy Manual, make (or delegate) hiring decisions, discipline decisions, pay decisions, employment termination decisions, evaluate job performance, and deal with all other personnel matters in consultation with the Senior Pastor and Executive Pastor.
(2) The Management Team shall recommend annual salary and benefits for the Church staff as part of the annual Church budget.

e. Special Task Forces and *ad hoc* Committees
Whenever the Management Team determines that special task forces/*ad hoc* committees need to be formed among the Church membership, the Management Team shall initiate an appropriate recommendation to the Nominating Committee which, in turn, shall make the necessary appointments to such special task force and/or *ad hoc* committee, including the appointment of a Chair-man. Once members are appointed to such special task force and/or *ad hoc* committee, they shall function under the direction of and in communication with, and report to, the Management Team.

2. Composition and Selection
   a. The Management Team shall be composed of twelve members of the Church.

   b. The Nominating Committee shall strive to nominate members for the Management Team who are not currently serving on the Deacon Ministry Team, the Equipping Ministry Team, or the Nominating Committee. On an annual basis, the Nominating Committee shall request recommendations for the Management Team from the members of the Church. Members of the Nominating Committee may also submit recommendations. Once the Nominating Committee has identified the names of potential nominees, the following procedures shall be observed:
      (1) The names of all potential nominees shall be submitted to the Pastoral Leadership Team for review. The members of the Pastoral Leadership Team may request a potential nominee's name be removed from the list if they believe that the nominee does not meet the spiritual qualifications for service.
      (2) Members of the Nominating Committee shall contact potential nominees to determine if they are willing to serve if elected. Potential nominees must indicate they believe that they meet the qualifications for service and are willing to serve.
      (3) The Chairman of the Nominating Committee shall appoint teams of two from the Nominating Committee to interview each potential nominee.
      (4) The Nominating Committee shall present information (picture, biographical sketch, testimony, etc.) to the members of the Church about each nominee willing to serve if elected, at least fourteen calendar days before the annual Church business conference in October. The number of nominees presented to the members of the Church shall be the exact number of persons needed for service.

   c. Members of the Pastoral Leadership Team may advise the Management Team but are not eligible to serve as members of the Management Team. Neither paid Church staff nor immediate family members (spouse, parents, and children) of the Pastoral Leadership Team or Church support staff shall be selected as members of the Management Team.

d. The Management Team shall elect its Officers from among its members on an annual basis.

3. Election
   a. The election of the Management Team shall be held during the annual Church business conference in October.[4] The vote shall be by secret ballot, with a "yes" and "no" by each nominee's name, and election shall require a three-fourths ($^3/_4$) affirmative vote of the members present and voting for election of such nominee to the Management Team. If a nominee is not elected, another nominee shall be submitted to the Church by the Nominating Committee as soon as feasible.

   b. If vacancies occur on the Management Team, the Management Team may decide to function with fewer members or fill the vacancy with a replacement of the Management Team's own choosing. Such replacement shall serve out the remainder of the unexpired term of the person he or she replaces.

4. Term
   The members of the Management Team shall serve three-year terms, on a rotating basis, beginning January 1 of each year, and shall not succeed themselves in office for two years.

5. Meetings
   The Management Team shall meet monthly or as necessary. A majority of the members of the Management Team shall constitute a quorum for the transaction of business, and action of the Management Team shall be approved by a three-fourths ($^3/_4$) affirmative vote of all the members of the Management Team.

C. Senior Pastor

1. Qualifications and Responsibilities
   a. The Senior Pastor shall be a man called of God and set apart to the gospel ministry, evangelical in theology, in accordance with the "Baptist Faith and Message" (2000 edition), and committed to living and serving in a manner consistent with the standards set forth in Scripture for such a leader.
   b. The Senior Pastor shall be called to lead the Church to understand, embrace, and accomplish its mission as defined by the primary biblical purposes of worship/magnification, evangelism/missions, fellowship/membership, discipleship/maturity, and service/ministry. The Senior Pastor leads the Church through his primary biblical roles of elder/overseer, evangelist, shepherd, preacher/teacher, and equipper.
   c. The specific responsibilities of the Senior Pastor may be outlined in terms of his primary biblical roles as follows:
      (1) Elder/Overseer–As elder/overseer, the Senior Pastor is the principal leader and vision caster of the Church (cf. Acts 20:28; Philippians 1:1; I Timothy 3:1-7; Titus 1:5-9; I Peter 5:1-4).
      (2) Evangelist–As evangelist, the Senior Pastor models the practice of personal evangelism incumbent on every believer and ensures that the Church is challenged and equipped to be obedient to the command of the Lord Jesus Christ to "make disciples" locally and globally (cf. II Timothy 4:5; Matthew 28:19).
      (3) Shepherd–As shepherd, the Senior Pastor models the heart of the Chief Shepherd and ensures that the Church is well led, cared for, fed, and protected (cf. Acts 20:28; I Peter 5:1-4).
      (4) Preacher/Teacher–As preacher/teacher, the Senior Pastor is the principal communicator of God's Word in public worship and ensures that the Church is growing to maturity in Christ through the Spirit-anointed teaching of sound doctrine (cf. Acts 6:4; Ephesians 4:11; II Timothy 4:1-4; Titus 1:9).
      (5) Equipper–As equipper, the Senior Pastor partners with other leaders to empower and equip maturing members for significant service and ministry by discovering, developing, and deploying their spiritual gifts (cf. Ephesians 4:12; II Timothy 2:2).

2. Composition and Selection
   a. In the selection of the Senior Pastor, a Senior Pastor Search Committee composed of three members from the Management Team and four members from the Church at large, plus two additional non-voting alternate members, shall be nominated by the Management Team, and elected at a scheduled or called Church business conference. Members of the Pastoral Leadership Team and their immediate family members (spouse, parents, and children) are not eligible to serve on the Senior Pastor Search Committee. The Senior Pastor Search Committee shall work to identify a Senior Pastor whose gifts, character, and calling fit him for that office. A majority of the members of the Senior Pastor Search Committee shall constitute a quorum for the transaction of business, and action of the Senior Pastor Search Committee shall be approved by a three-fourths ($^3/_4$) affirmative vote of all the members of the Senior Pastor Search Committee present and voting.
   b. The selection of the Senior Pastor shall occur at a Church business conference called specifically for that purpose. No name shall be considered or nominated except as recommended by the Senior Pastor Search Committee. The vote for the Senior Pastor shall be by secret ballot, with a "yes" and "no," and shall require a three-fourths ($^3/_4$) affirmative vote of the members present and voting for election. If the recommendation of the Senior Pastor Search Committee does not receive the required three-fourths ($^3/_4$) affirmative vote, the Senior Pastor Search Committee shall continue its duties and shall present another recommendation to the Church.

3. Term

   The Senior Pastor shall serve at the pleasure of the Church and under continuing call until the Church or the Senior Pastor requests otherwise. Resignation of the Senior Pastor shall require thirty days prior written notice to the Church. Termination of the services and employment of the Senior Pastor shall require a two-thirds ($^2/_3$) affirmative vote of those members present and voting for such motion at a Church business conference called specifically for that purpose.

D. Other Church Staff

Church staff shall be employed subject to the terms and conditions set forth in the Church's Personnel Policy Manual.

1. Pastoral Leadership Team
   a. All Pastoral Leadership Team members shall be considered pastors and shall function in similar roles as those stated for the Senior Pastor in Section III.C.1. They shall be called of God into the gospel ministry, and are expected to be evangelical in theology, in accordance with the "Baptist Faith and Message" (2000 edition), and committed to living and serving in a manner consistent with the standards set forth in Scripture for such leaders. In evaluating the job performance of these pastors, the Senior Pastor and the Executive Pastor shall work with the Personnel subcommittee of the Management Team as stated in Section III.B.1.d. The Executive Pastor shall be evaluated by the Senior Pastor and the Personnel subcommittee of the Management Team.
   b. All Pastoral Leadership Team positions shall be determined by the Senior Pastor and approved by the Management Team. All members of the Pastoral Leadership Team are selected by the Senior Pastor and the Management Team, approved by the Church, and shall be accountable to the Senior Pastor. The vote for a Pastoral Leadership Team member shall be by secret ballot, with a "yes" and "no," and shall require a three-fourths ($^3/_4$) affirmative vote of the members present and voting for election. The services and employment of a member of the Pastoral Leadership Team may be terminated upon the recommendation of the Senior Pastor to, and approval by, the Management Team. If the position of the Senior Pastor is vacant, the Executive Pastor and the Chairman of the Management Team shall jointly function in that capacity for this limited purpose.
2. Church Support Staff

   All other Church support staff positions shall be determined by the Senior Pastor and approved by the Management Team. All members of the Church support staff shall be selected by, are accountable to, and serve at the discretion of the Executive Pastor in consultation with the Personnel subcommittee of the Management Team. In the absence of the Executive Pastor, the

Personnel subcommittee of the Management Team shall function in this supervisory role.

SECTION IV — MINISTRY LEADERSHIP TEAMS

A. Deacon Ministry Team

1. Qualifications and Responsibilities
   a. The Deacon Ministry Team shall include men who are members of the Church, exemplary in their conduct, discreet in judgment, of honest report, full of faith and conscious that they shall set worthy examples of cooperation, love and loyalty for all members of the Church, abiding by the principles set forth in Acts 6 and I Timothy 3.
   b. The Deacon Ministry Team shall promote peace, harmony, and a spirit of unity and cooperation among the membership of the Church.
   c. The Deacon Ministry Team shall serve the body in the following areas:
      (1) Pastoral support (i.e., evangelism, new member follow-up, hospital visitation, nursing home visitation, homebound, bereavement, etc.);
      (2) Church ordinance administration (Lord's Supper shall be observed at least quarterly);
      (3) Benevolence ministry administration;
      (4) Conflict resolution; and,
      (5) Leadership for new or existing ministries which are consistent with the respective deacon's gifts and calling to ministry.
   d. When the office of Senior Pastor is vacant, the Deacon Officers shall consult with the Pastoral Leadership Team and are responsible for coordinating pulpit supply speakers and recommending an interim pastor to the members of the Church.
2. Composition and Selection
   a. The Deacon Ministry Team shall determine the number of men necessary to function effectively in its various ministries.
   b. The Nominating Committee shall strive to nominate members for the Deacon Ministry Team who are not currently serving on the Management Team, the Equipping Ministry Team, or the Nominating Committee. On an annual basis, the Nominating Committee shall

request recommendations for the Deacon Ministry Team from members of the Church. Members of the Nominating Committee may also submit recommendations. Once the committee has identified the names of potential nominees, the following procedures shall be observed:

(1) The names of all potential nominees shall be submitted to the Pastoral Leadership Team for review. The members of the Pastoral Leadership Team may request a potential nominee's name be removed from the list if they believe that the nominee does not meet the spiritual qualifications for service.

(2) Members of the Nominating Committee shall contact potential nominees to determine if they are willing to serve if elected. Potential nominees must indicate they believe that they meet the qualifications for service and are willing to serve.

(3) A Chairman-appointed member of the Nominating Committee and a Deacon officer shall interview each potential nominee.

(4) The Nominating Committee shall submit information (picture, biographical sketch, testimony, etc.) to the members of the Church about each nominee willing to serve if elected, at least fourteen calendar days before the annual Church business conference in October. The number of nominees presented shall be the exact number of persons needed for service.

c. The Deacon Ministry Team shall elect its officers from among its members on an annual basis.

3. Election

a. The election of the Deacon Ministry Team shall be held at the annual Church business conference in October.[5] The vote shall be by secret ballot, with a "yes" and "no" by each nominee's name, and shall require a three-fourths ($^3/_4$) affirmative vote of the members present and voting for election of such nominee to the Deacon Ministry Team. If a nominee is not elected, another nominee shall be submitted to the Church by the Nominating Committee as soon as feasible.

b. If vacancies occur on the Deacon Ministry Team, the Deacon Ministry Team may decide to function with fewer members or fill the vacancy with a replacement of the Deacon Ministry Team's own choosing. Such replacement shall serve out the remainder of the unexpired term of the person he replaces.

4. Term

Members of the Deacon Ministry Team shall serve three-year terms, on a rotating basis, beginning January 1 of each year, and shall not succeed themselves in office for at least two years.

5. Meetings

There shall be regular meetings as determined by the Deacon Officers. A majority of the members of the Deacon Ministry Team shall constitute a quorum for the transaction of business, and action of the Deacon Ministry Team shall be approved by a majority vote of the members of the Deacon Ministry Team present and voting.

B. Equipping Ministry Team

1. Qualifications and Responsibilities
   a. The Equipping Ministry Team shall include men and women who are members of the Church, exemplary in their conduct, discreet in judgment, of honest report, full of faith, and conscious that they shall set worthy examples of cooperation, love, and loyalty for all members of the Church.
   b. The Equipping Ministry Team shall work with an appropriate Pastoral Leadership Team sponsor to develop ministry teams to mobilize members of the Church for ministry.
   c. The Equipping Ministry Team shall identify, recruit, equip, lead, and deploy others to be involved in various ministries of the Church, with no time placed on their involvement.

2. Composition and Selection
   a. The Equipping Ministry Team shall be composed of nine members of the Church.
   b. The Nominating Committee shall strive to nominate members for the Equipping Ministry Team who are not currently serving on the Management Team, the Deacon Ministry Team, or the Nominating Committee. On an annual basis, the Nominating Committee shall request recommendations from the members of the Church. Members

of the Nominating Committee may also submit recommendations. Once the committee has identified the names of potential nominees, the following procedures shall be observed:

(1) The names of all potential nominees shall be submitted to the Pastoral Leadership Team for review. The members of the Pastoral Leadership Team may request a potential nominee's name be removed from the list if they believe that the nominee does not meet the spiritual qualifications for service.

(2) Members of the Nominating Committee shall contact potential nominees to determine if they are willing to serve if elected. Potential nominees must indicate they believe that they meet the qualifications for service and are willing to serve.

(3) The Chairman of the Nominating Committee shall appoint teams of two from the Nominating Committee to interview each potential nominee.

(4) The Nominating Committee shall submit information (picture, biographical sketch, testimony, etc.) to the members of the Church about each nominee willing to serve if elected, at least fourteen calendar days before the annual Church business conference in October. The number of nominees presented shall be the exact number of persons needed for service.

c. The Equipping Ministry Team shall elect its officers from among its members on an annual basis.

3. Election

a. The election shall be held at the annual Church business conference in October. The vote shall be by secret ballot, with a "yes" and "no" by each nominee's name, and election shall require a three-fourths ($^3/_4$) affirmative vote of the members present and voting for election to the Equipping Ministry Team. If a nominee is not elected, another nominee shall be submitted to the Church by the Nominating Committee as soon as feasible.

b. If vacancies occur on the Equipping Ministry Team, the Equipping Ministry Team may decide to function with fewer members or fill the vacancy with a replacement of the Equipping Ministry Team's own choosing. Such replacement shall serve out the remainder of the unexpired term of the person he or she replaces.

4. Term
   The members of the Equipping Ministry Team shall serve three-year terms, on a rotating basis, beginning January 1 of each year, and shall not succeed themselves in office for at least two years.

5. Meetings
   Meetings of the Equipping Ministry Team shall be determined by the Chairman and an appropriate Pastoral Leadership Team sponsor. A majority of the members of the Equipping Ministry Team shall constitute a quorum for the transaction of business, and action of the Equipping Ministry Team shall be approved by a majority vote of the members of the Equipping Ministry Team present and voting.

SECTION V — Nominating Committee

A. Qualifications and Responsibilities

The Nominating Committee shall be composed of men and women who are members of the Church, exemplary in their conduct, discreet in judgment, of honest report, full of faith, and conscious that they shall set worthy examples of cooperation, love and loyalty for all members of the Church.

The Nominating Committee shall select nominees for the Management Team, the Equipping Ministry Team, and the Deacon Ministry Team in accordance with the procedures set forth above in these Bylaws.

B. Composition and Selection

The Nominating Committee shall be composed of the Senior Pastor, Chairman of the Management Team, and nine members of the Church at-large.

1. The Management Team and the Senior Pastor shall identify potential nominees for the Nominating Committee from the members of the Church. An effort shall be made to ensure that such nominees represent a broad cross-section of the Church. The Senior Pastor and the Management Team shall

strive to select members for the Nominating Committee who are not currently serving on the Management Team, the Deacon Ministry Team, or the Equipping Ministry Team.

2. The Management Team shall submit names of all potential nominees for the Nominating Committee to the Pastoral Leadership Team for review. The members of the Pastoral Leadership Team may request a potential nominee's name be removed from the list if they believe that the nominee does not meet the spiritual qualifications for service.
3. Members of the Management Team shall contact potential nominees to determine if they are willing to serve if elected. Potential nominees must indicate that they believe they meet the spiritual qualifications for service and are willing to serve if elected.
4. The Chairman of the Management Team shall appoint teams of two from the Management Team to interview each potential nominee.
5. The Management Team shall submit information (picture, biographical sketch, testimony, etc.) to the members of the Church about each nominee willing to serve if elected, at least fourteen calendar days before the annual Church business conference in October. The number of nominees presented shall be the exact number of persons needed for service.
6. The Chairman of the Nominating Committee shall be appointed by the Management Team.

C. Election

1. The election of the Nominating Committee shall be held during the annual Church business conference in October.[6] The vote shall be by secret ballot, with a "yes" and "no" by each nominee's name, and election shall require a three-fourths ($^3/_4$) affirmative vote of the members present and voting for election of such nominee to the Nominating Committee. If a nominee is not elected, another nominee shall be submitted to the Church by the Nominating Committee as soon as feasible.
2. If vacancies occur on the Nominating Committee, the Nominat-ing Committee may decide to function with fewer members or fill the vacancy with a replacement of the Nominating Committee's own choosing. Such replacement shall serve out the remainder of the unexpired term of the person he or she replaces.

D. Term

The members of the Nominating Committee shall serve three-year terms, on a rotating basis, beginning January 1 of each year, and shall not succeed themselves in office for at least two years.

E. Meetings

The Nominating Committee shall meet monthly or as necessary. A majority of the members of the Nominating Committee shall constitute a quorum for the transaction of business, and action of the Nominating Committee shall be approved by a majority vote of the members of the Nominating Committee present and voting.

SECTION VI — Finance

A. Annual Budget

1. The members of the Church shall approve the next year's budget during the annual Church business conference in October by a two-thirds ($^2/_3$) affirmative majority of the members present and voting. The votes shall be counted by members of the Management Team.
2. The members of the Church shall approve non-budgeted expenditures exceeding an annual cumulative total of three percent (3%) of the annual budget by a two-thirds ($^2/_3$) affirmative majority of the members present and voting. This shall not apply in emergency situations to monies previously set aside in a maintenance reserve fund.
3. The members of the Church shall approve all budget reallocations exceeding an annual cumulative total of three percent (3%) of the annual budget by a two-thirds ($^2/_3$) affirmative majority of the members present and voting.

B. Church Financial Statements

1. The Church shall distribute to members of the Church written quarterly financial reports on Sunday morning of the regularly scheduled Church business conferences.
2. The Church shall distribute to members of the Church written reports of non-budgeted expenditures exceeding an annual cumulative total of two percent (2%) of the annual budget.

C. **Acquisition of Land, Buildings, Borrowing of Funds, Sale of Property**
The members of the Church shall approve all acquisition of land, buildings, borrowing of funds, and sale of property by a two-thirds (2/3) affirmative vote of the Church members present and voting for such motion at any Church business conference.

D. **Audit of Church Finances**
The Management Team shall be responsible for selecting an independent Certified Public Accountant to audit the Church's finances annually. The auditor shall not be a member of the Church. The scope of services provided by the independent Certified Public Accountant shall be determined by the Management Team.

E. **Financial Integrity of the Church**

1. The Management Team shall be accountable to the Church for maintaining the financial integrity of all the financial activities of the Church. The Management Team shall establish operating and reserve funds that are adequate to operate the Church efficiently. The Management Team shall report the prior year's results and the disposition of any budget surplus annually to the Church. If anticipated receipts are less than the annual budget, the Management Team will make the necessary changes in the annual budget to operate within the anticipated receipts.
2. The Management Team and the Officers of the Church having access to funds of the Church shall be bonded in such amounts as the Management Team determines, from time to time.

F. **Financial Policies and Procedures**
The Management Team shall develop and approve written financial policies and procedures for all financial activities of the Church and all related activities. The Management Team shall be accountable to the Church as follows:

1. The Management Team shall approve non-budgeted expenditures not to exceed an annual cumulative total of three percent (3%) of the annual budget.
2. The Management Team shall approve budget reallocations not to exceed an annual cumulative total of three percent (3%) of the annual budget.

3. The Management Team shall receive and approve detailed monthly financial statements for the Church.

SECTION VII — Records and Reports

The Church shall maintain and keep the following records and reports in the Church office:

1. An accounting system that provides financial records with actual and detailed information on receipts, disbursements, balances, and the financial condition of the Church;
2. Written minutes of all Church business conferences and all Management Team meetings;
3. A listing of the Church's real and personal property, fixed assets, and insurance records;
4. A record of the members of the Church, listing the names and addresses of all members;
5. Annual contribution statements for all contributors; and,
6. A certified written report from the independent Certified Public Accountant on the annual audit of the Church.

SECTION VIII — Maintenance

A. Year End

The Church shall operate on a calendar year with respect to operation of the budget and for committee and team service.

B. Policies and Procedures Manual

The Executive Pastor shall be responsible for compiling and maintaining a Policies and Procedures Manual for the day-to-day administrative functions of the Church not covered in the Constitution and Bylaws. Subjects covered in the Policies and Procedures Manual shall include, but are not limited to:

1. Personnel policies and procedures;
2. Financial policies and procedures;
3. Church property policies and procedures; and,
4. Child protection policies.

The Policies and Procedures Manual shall be available in the office of the Executive Pastor for review by members of the Church. Any suggested changes shall be recommended in writing to, and decided upon by, the Management Team.

SECTION IX — Adoption and Amendment of Bylaws

A. Adoption

These Bylaws shall be adopted by a two-thirds (2/3) affirmative vote of the members of the Church present and voting at the duly called Church business conference at which these Bylaws are submitted for adoption.[7]

B. Amendment

These Bylaws may be amended by a two-thirds (2/3) affirmative vote of the members of the Church present and voting at any Church business conference. Any proposal to amend these Bylaws shall be brought to the attention of the Management Team at least thirty calendar days before it appears on the agenda of any Church business conference.

C. Records

A copy of the most recent edition of the Bylaws shall at all times be kept with the records of the Church. A copy of the Constitution and Bylaws shall be made available to any Church member upon request.

ENDNOTES

Note: The following Endnotes are part of the Constitution and Bylaws and shall have full force and effect. (O.C.G.A. stands for "Official Code of Georgia Annotated.")

1- This Constitution and Bylaws shall become effective immediately upon adoption by the members of the Church, and shall supersede and replace the existing Constitution and Bylaws of Mountain Park First Baptist Church, Inc. Following the adoption of the Constitution and Bylaws, the Executive Pastor is authorized to make any and all necessary clerical corrections and typographical corrections to the Constitution and Bylaws.

The provisions of the Constitution and Bylaws shall prevail and control over any conflicting resolutions or actions taken by any other ecclesiastical body and over any conflicting resolutions or actions taken by any employee of the Church, the Management Team, the Pastoral Leadership Team, the Deacon Ministry Team, and/or any other committee, subcommittee, or team, which are not in conformity with the Constitution and Bylaws.

2- In the event a religious doctrine of the Church is inconsistent with any provision of the Georgia Nonprofit Code, or other law, the religious doctrine of the Church shall control to the fullest extent permitted by applicable law.

3- The Board of Directors and the Officers of the Church shall, to the fullest extent permitted by applicable law, be entitled to indemnification and advances and reimbursements for expenses, in accordance with O.C.G.A Section 14-3-850 through O.C.G.A. Section 14-3-858.

4- In order to ensure a smooth transition of Church business, the persons serving on the Board of Trustees, the Personnel Committee, and the Finance Committee of the Church on May 21, 2006, shall continue to serve and shall constitute the Management Team and the Board of Directors of the Church, and such Management Team shall elect the Officers of the Church. In October 2007, in the annual Church business conference, the first new members (4) of the Management Team shall be elected to serve three-year terms beginning January 1, 2008. The original Management Team, having been given one, two and three year terms by the Nominating Committee, will begin rotating off on January 1, 2008, according to their assigned terms.

5- In order to maintain the continuity of the deacon ministry, the deacons serving as of May 21, 2006, shall continue to serve as the Deacon Ministry Team. In the October 2006 annual Church business conference, by the process described in Section IV.A. of these Bylaws, the Church will elect the appropriate number of deacons to replace those scheduled to rotate off of the Deacon Ministry Team. These newly elected deacons will assume their duties on January 1, 2007.

6- Upon approval of these Bylaws, the persons serving on the Nominating Committee of the Church as of May 21, 2006, shall assume the duties of the Nominating Committee as described in Section V. of these Bylaws (with the exception of nominating new members of the Management Team in October 2006). A new Nominating Committee will be elected in a timely manner in accordance with Section V. of these Bylaws and will assume its full responsibilities and duties on January 1, 2007.

7- All amendments to the Articles of Incorporation of Mountain Park First Baptist Church, Inc., necessary to conform the current Articles of Incorporation of Mountain Park First Baptist Church, Inc., to this Constitution and Bylaws are hereby approved and the Management Team, acting as the Board of Directors of the Church, and the Officers of the Church, are authorized to prepare, execute, and file any and all necessary documents and Articles of Amendment to the Articles of Incorporation of Mountain Park First Baptist Church, Inc.

Chapter Five

The Big Four

In the previous chapter we looked at the four different lay leadership groups I call The Big Four. Terminology may vary, but the essential key to developing a proper and effective biblical church structure is this—forming these four lay leadership groups. We have looked at them briefly, but let me make a few salient points to help you get the big picture of how these four entities should function biblically and practically.

THE EQUIPPING MINISTRY TEAM

The purpose of the Equipping Ministry Team (EMT) is *to recruit church members to servant leadership in the various ministries and programs of the church.* The EMT helps men and women find places where they will love serving, and in which they can find great fulfillment. It's in this sense that individuals of the EMT function as personal consultants to members, helping match up their gifting and interests with the needs of the ministry.

One of the primary instruments to help them is the SHAPE document. You'll find a model of this in Appendix #3. This tool helps assess one's spiritual giftedness, heart or passion, natural abilities, personality and life experiences so that person will know which ministry would be a good fit for them. For this to work well, it's important that church members complete their SHAPE profile and that the results be entered into a database.

Many church software programs allow one to enter user-defined profile codes for members. Each item on the SHAPE document can be assigned a profile code. When a ministry within the church calls for a person with certain attributes, the database can run a report of the desired codes to identify potential ministry participants.[1] The EMT will also find it helpful to coordinate their efforts with appropriate member(s) of the PLT in recommending people to serve in a variety of church programs; i.e., teachers, choir directors, leaders for children and youth ministries, etc.

The congregation doesn't need to vote on any of these positions at a church business conference, or require people to rotate off, especially if they are doing their job well and loving it. Often it is helpful to initially ask people for a one-year commitment to a ministry area. After that year, an EMT member would help the member reevaluate if he or she wishes to continue in that area. As such, the members of the EMT need to help people find their favorite thing to do in the church, a place of service where they can be effective and happy. To help them do this, the EMT will need to maintain a "Ministry Discovery Handbook," which will have a complete listing of every ministry option.[2]

THE DEACON MINISTRY TEAM

There is no question that the office of deacon is central to the New Testament. In fact, it's one of only two offices cited in the life of the early church (see chapter 8), and yet you will have a hard time finding a truly effective deacon ministry in our churches today. As you might well imagine, this has caused many pastors and lay people to throw their hands up in despair.

It has already been established in chapter 4 that the key responsibility of the Deacon Ministry Team (DMT) is *to provide the lay pastoral care backbone of the church.* The biblical admonition is that the deacons must be ministry-centered, not business-centered. They must let another lay leadership group take care of the business of the church, or else they will lapse into a "board" mentality, taking care of things like finances and personnel issues, rather than functioning as spiritual leaders.

Before I share with you an exciting, biblically-principled plan that will establish an effective deacon ministry in your church, let's review seven current but poor options for deacon ministry:

- First, deacons are assigned to different small groups or Sunday school classes. But when this happens, the deacons lose their unique identity, and they begin to serve simply as managers or coordinators for ministry. Then there is also the problem numerically and logistically of lining up deacons with the various classes.
- Second, deacons are organized simply around ministry teams. The main problem here is that deacons can become a bottleneck for ministry.
- Third, the deacons function as chairmen of all the church committees. Aside from the logistical problems, the primary concern here is that the deacons become like a clearinghouse for all church business, thus ignoring their calling to be the pastoral care leaders of the church.
- Fourth, the deacons run the church by functioning as a "board." This option is extremely unhealthy and not biblically based.
- Fifth is an elder system of government, wherein the elders are considered the true spiritual leaders of the church. This relegates the deacons to the routine and mundane assignments of the church rather than primarily to pastoral care matters.
- A sixth option is one that grows out of despair and frustration: Let there be no deacons in the church since God has called all of His people to get involved in ministry.
- Seventh is the option known as "The Deacon Family Ministry Plan,"[3] whereby the deacons are assigned and responsible to minister to ten families. But there are several major problems with this arrangement too.

  First of all, the ratio of one deacon for each ten families is unrealistic. For instance, particularly in large churches, if this ratio is maintained, the number of members serving on the DMT would be unmanageably large. So, as a "corrective," here is what usually happens: The ratio is changed by assigning many more families to each deacon.

  Then a second problem emerges: The deacons soon find that they don't have the time to minister to 30 or 40 or 50 families and still function well at work during the week!

  A third problem that surfaces is that the deacons are expected to meet a wide variety of ministry needs among all of their families, when the fact of the matter is they are SHAPE'd best to serve effectively within a more narrow range of ministries.

  Fourth, and most importantly, the Deacon Family Ministry Plan is

> simply unbiblical. For instance, in the sixth chapter of the book of Acts, we read that only seven men were selected to serve as deacons, and yet the membership of that early church was already in the thousands by that time. Just do the math. What was that ratio of deacons to families?

The key to understanding a proper biblical model for deacon ministry is to recognize that deacons are not only spiritual managers, they are also spiritual mentors. As mentors they can head up Deacon-Led Ministry Teams[4] so that even more ministry occurs. For instance, they can lead lay teams to help out with:

- Outreach
- New member follow-up
- Nursing home ministry
- The bereaved
- Widows
- Prayer needs
- Hospital visitation

Other deacon-led teams can be formed as well, depending on how God guides your particular DMT. For more ideas, please see the Deacon Handbook found in Appendix #1.

Although you're free to get very creative at this point, let me give you just one example—a Deacon-Led Hospital Ministry Team. This team, led by two deacons (a leader and an assistant), with help from the EMT and PLT, would put together a group of 30 or more men and women from within the church. These individuals would then coordinate their hospital visits, each person taking just one day a month. If you do this, those within your congregation will be cared for on a daily basis and by different people.

For those of us who labor in smaller churches, where there isn't a full-time Minister of Pastoral Care, I would like to suggest that you invite a hospital chaplain to equip the members of your Deacon-Led Hospital Ministry Team. The hospital chaplain can teach them exactly how to conduct an effective hospital visit. I think you can begin to see how the sky is the limit at this point of getting large numbers of people involved in ministry, and this is important because most Christians have a passion to serve the Lord in ways that provide fulfillment and significance.

If the DMT leaders are properly equipped and consulted, I can't think of any weaknesses to this approach. To the contrary, I can think of several important advantages. Let me list seven of them for you:

- Almost everyone in the life of our churches can minister—male, female, married, widowed, single and divorced. Would you not agree that when people are visited and prayed for in the hospitals, they don't care about those kinds of matters?
- The members of the DMT don't become a bottleneck for ministry. Rather, they enlarge it by mentoring others in a variety of ministries.
- Ministry needs are met in multiplied ways, far beyond what just the members of the PLT and DMT could do alone.
- The non-ordained of our churches can get vitally involved in ministry too.
- This arrangement is more similar to what we find in Acts 6 in terms of the ratio of deacons to the number of Christians.
- Each current member of the DMT would be involved in no more than two deacon-led ministries, thus allowing him to minister well by focusing on those areas in which he is especially gifted and motivated to serve.
- The deacons won't be overwhelmed with unrealistic expectations. Their responsibilities are manageable.

When the members of the DMT enlist and equip others,[5] everyone wins. This also assists the members of the PLT in seeing that ministry occurs. This is the biblical model. Everyone can have the fun of being a minister!

THE MANAGEMENT TEAM

There is yet a third very important lay leadership group that needs to be formed in order to develop an effective biblical church structure. In our congregation, we call it the Management Team (MT), but it could also be called by a variety of other names.[6] This group is to *exercise oversight in the management and governance of the church; i.e., administrating, directing, guiding and leading the business affairs of the church.* Some churches may choose for this entity to be comprised of men only, but we've opted for this group to be made up of both men and women, and our rationale is given in the Management Team Handbook found in Appendix #1.

The four principal responsibilities of the MT are to:

- Provide accountability for the Senior Pastor
- Ensure the financial integrity of the church
- Develop and adopt policies related to the operation of the church
- Supervise the personnel matters of the church

In short, the MT functions as the Board of Directors, thereby handling all of the corporate issues, legal affairs and business matters of the church. These responsibilities are administered through the following three sub-committees, each comprised of roughly one-third of the MT members:

- Finance subcommittee
- Personnel subcommittee
- Policy and Legal Issues subcommittee

THE NOMINATING COMMITTEE

The final lay leadership group that needs to be formed in order to develop an effective biblical church structure is the Nominating Committee (NC). The NC is composed of the Senior Pastor, the chairman of the MT, and nine members elected by the church.[7] Historically, during the church's infancy, the apostles or apostolically trained men such as Timothy appointed the earliest church leaders. At that stage, they didn't need a nominating process. But with the era of the apostles long since past, our churches of today need a process for the ongoing selection of our leaders.

Though it could be argued that what I'm proposing isn't truly biblical, it is biblically principled. I'm suggesting a NC probably quite unlike any that you have known before, however. Its assignment is crucial, but its focus is very narrow; its job is to *recommend capable church members to fill the openings in only the EMT, DMT and MT.* You will recall that the Equipping Ministry Team (EMT) will recruit church members to leadership in most of the other various ministries and church programs.

In the biblical structure I'm proposing, there's a sense in which the direction of the church rests with the NC more than with any other entity. They're the ones who select, evaluate, and interview the nominees for the three other important lay leadership groups (EMT, DMT, MT). If their choices are less than stellar, the church will suffer. If their choices are excellent, the church will be blessed. That is, no church structure, however biblical, will be effective unless the leaders are godly and competent.

OBLIGATIONS OF THE BIG FOUR

While it's true that the congregation follows democratic processes by prayerfully electing those who lead them, these leaders are then obligated to seek the mind and heart of Christ in all of their decisions. In this sense, the church isn't a pure, straightforward democracy. It's a Christocracy.

In Appendix #1, you'll find four important handbooks that will prove very useful in recruiting individuals to serve in these lay leadership groups. The NC handbook will suggest a time line for this process. Eventually these groups in a given church will want to develop their own operating manuals with their own slant. In individual churches each group will probably function a little differently than a group by the same name in another church.

1. An example of how our church coded the SHAPE attributes to our church management software is found in Appendix #4.

2. Every ministry team and/or committee will be represented by a one-page document within the "Ministry Discovery Handbook," giving the name of each particular ministry, a purpose statement, a description and who serves on it, and identify the primary PLT resource person(s). Such a tool will assist the EMT greatly in helping to set up each ministry, as well as avoid duplication among various ministries. An excellent resource to use at this point is *The Equipping Church Guidebook,* by Sue Mallory and Brad Smith, Grand Rapids, Michigan, Zondervan, 2001.

3. *The Deacon Family Ministry Plan,* Charles F. Treadway, 1974, Convention Press, revised, 1977.

4. Not all deacon ministry teams need to be deacon-led, however. For instance, in chapter nine of this book (Church Conflict), reference will be made to a Conciliation Team within the DMT. In my estimation, this Conciliation Team should not be deacon-led, but should be comprised only of those members currently serving on the DMT.

5. Since all of the deacon-led ministry teams are, quite obviously, ministry teams, they will need to be included in the Ministry Discovery Handbook maintained by the EMT, and they will simply need to be flagged as deacon-led.

6. Other examples might be Administrative Leadership Team (ALT), Strategic Leadership Team (SLT), Board of Overseers, or Board of Directors.

7. See Constitution and Bylaws, Section V.

Chapter Six

Orientation for the Big Four

Regardless of when a congregation schedules its church business conference(s), there will be a certain time in the year when its main leadership will need to be elected. You'll remember that we're referring to these four lay leadership groups as The Big Four, which are the:

- Equipping Ministry Team
- Deacon Ministry Team
- Management Team
- Nominating Committee

I would recommend the annual church business conference as being the ideal time for electing these men and women to serve on these teams. In our church, as is typical of most, this election occurs in the fall. A church that follows a fiscal year instead of a calendar year might want its election cycle to mirror the fiscal year.

Once these teams have been formed, you'll need to coach them in their new roles. Pick a time soon after the elections and right before personal schedules get hectic because of the holidays. Encourage their spouses to attend as well so their spouses will have a greater appreciation for everything that will be involved in their ministry. Make it an event to remember, and then transition into a work mode.

Begin with a large group meeting, taking about 20 minutes. In the Orientation Guide (Appendix #2), you'll see the material that we cover in this session. The beauty of it is that the entire group is exposed to the big picture to see how and why the church is organized as it is.

After getting the big picture and seeing how their particular team fits in, each of these four groups breaks away for a time of specialized training. A member of the PLT and the outgoing chairman of that particular team should lead these breakout groups. They should go over much more comprehensive material specific to their own team and present members with their own handbooks (You'll find these handbooks in Appendix #1.) and operating manuals.

So, right after the new year begins, every newly elected individual will be ready to hit the ground running on his or her new assignment. Everyone's coached and set to go!

Chapter Seven

Church Business Conferences

Probably the vast majority of Christians in virtually every type of congregation look upon church business conferences with utter boredom. It shouldn't be this way. We need to develop an atmosphere in these meetings that would inspire, encourage and motivate our members to an even greater commitment to Christ, whether the meetings occur on a monthly, quarterly or annual basis.

In our congregation, these church business conferences occur on a quarterly basis, and we call them our **SALT & SPICE** nights, acronyms that stand for the two parts of the meeting:

Strategic
Advanced
Leadership
Training
and
Significant
Promotion
Inspiration
Communication
Experience

During **SALT** we have an abbreviated worship service that also includes a short message on leadership. During **SPICE**, where the three operative words are in the middle, we do a variety of important things. Under **P**romotion we talk about key upcoming events. People are often down on what they are not up on, so this gives us an opportunity to apprise our people about important future events. Under **I**nspiration various members of the PLT help our church honor three different laypersons within our church with different awards, all of which are kept top secret until the actual moment the award is presented. These awards are:

- Whatever It Takes Award—This is an award that's presented to someone who has served the Lord effectively in the recent past in some unusual way, far above and beyond the call of duty.
- Service Recognition Award—Our churches are usually filled with many people who have served the Lord faithfully over a long period of time and in one particular ministry. This is a great time to honor them for this achievement.
- Sunday School Recognition Award—This award is usually presented to an individual or class that has experienced some kind of recent, outward success.

This is almost always the highlight of the entire service, and it provides a wonderful medium through which to recognize our laypersons on a regular basis. Please keep in mind that this may be one of the only times in a person's entire life that he or she is commended and celebrated in such a manner! It's at this point that we're also fulfilling the admonition to "stir up love and good works…exhorting one another" (Hebrews 10:24–25) within the life of the church. It's not unusual to see tears of joy on the faces of the recipients, along with affirmation and applause from members of the congregation.

These awards are coordinated by the members of the PLT, but it's always such a blessing to get private, unsolicited nominations from the congregation. I would advise you not to recognize more than one person for each award, though, so that the recognitions don't become perfunctory.

Finally, under **C**ommunication our congregation is actually called into church business conference. By this time a positive spiritual climate should have been established so that the business of the church can now be conducted in an atmosphere that will truly honor the Lord Jesus Christ.

There are many important matters within the constitution and bylaws (see chapter 4) on which I wish I could comment because they were so carefully and prayerfully considered and debated when they were drafted. This is especially true when it comes to church business conferences. You'll need to very carefully work your own way through these documents, but let me offer just a few very salient points for your consideration.

First, *there will be matters you will want to present to the congregation as reports.* This free flow of information is always helpful, especially when provided as handouts. But, unless unusual circumstances such as church discipline or church dissolution apply, there are only five major items upon which the congregation routinely needs to vote. This really does simplify church business conferences by reducing the items that need to be voted on by the congregation. It also empowers and releases ministries to make their own decisions (within authorized parameters) without having to get church approval for everything. The five important matters requiring church approval are

- The calling of the Senior Pastor, as well as other members of the PLT.
- The election of nominees to The Big Four at the annual church business conference. When electing leaders, it's quite common for congregants to vote from a slate of candidates greater than the number of leaders actually needed. You'll quickly see that the proposed selection process presented here does not follow such a system, and for the following reasons.

  First, whenever a congregation votes from a slate greater than the number of leaders needed, the church is setting itself up for "winners" and "losers," an all too common practice that serves no positive purpose.

  Second, the proposed process by which leaders are nominated, recruited and equipped is so thorough and biblically based that virtually every person on the ballot should be more than qualified to be elected.

  Third, when a slate of candidates greater than the number of leaders necessary is presented to the church for a vote, it's only natural that those who are more visible and well-known will be elected, whereas those with less of a "platform presence" are often overlooked.

  Fourth, in the highly unlikely event that the entire selection process is scandalous, the final vote is still with the congregation, and in our case the vote must be overwhelmingly positive (75% affirmative vote by secret ballot).

- The budget at the annual church business conference.
- Changes to the constitution and bylaws.
- Purchase and disposition of property.

Second, *all matters requiring church approval must be presented to the members of the MT at least 30 days before they can be placed on the agenda.* This doesn't mean that the members of the MT must be in agreement with the particular agenda item. It simply means that they must be able to know about it in order to study its implications. Such a stipulation prevents unnecessary and unpleasant surprises.

Gone are the days when a member or a group of members can bring up unscheduled items from the floor, after inviting large numbers of church members—many of whom may not have attended a church business conference in years—to vote along "party lines." It also means that when the agenda items are completed, the moderator states that the business meeting agenda is now finished, and he can then entertain a motion to adjourn.

Under this system, it would be impossible for the moderator to say, "Now does *anyone* have *anything* else they would like to bring up at this meeting?" Quite often, those words give microphone time to the most carnal members in our churches. A negative person may be able to garner influence when there is no set agenda determined beforehand. In that type of a forum, a carnal person is given an opportunity to create doubt and dissension, and this will sometimes destroy the harmony of a church in a matter of minutes.

Furthermore, in a church business conference where there are no predetermined agenda items and the members of the congregation are allowed to talk about anything, decisions are often based on the popularity of the speaker rather than on the merits of an idea. This brings reproach to the name of the Lord Jesus Christ and His church.

Third, *in my estimation, it is best that the Senior Pastor not serve as the moderator of these church business conferences* for several reasons. Most importantly, as moderator he would not be able to take part in the discussion. As a participant, however, he would then be free to speak to crucial issues on the occasions the discussion would benefit from his input. (You'll note in the bylaws of my current church that the chairman of the Management Team serves as moderator.)

For many of you, knowing and implementing just these three suggestions in your church business conferences would more than be worth the price of this book.

Now a closing comment about frequency. Many churches conduct their business conferences on a monthly basis and on a Wednesday night. Under such an arrangement, unfortunately, those who lead other midweek ministries are often unable to attend. Usually, only a very small fraction of the members are present. Under a proper church structure, however, there's no real need for a congregation to gather monthly to make church-wide business decisions. I'd suggest having regularly scheduled church conferences no more often than quarterly. Do them on a Sunday night, using the **SALT & SPICE** arrangement discussed in this chapter. This permits more people to be included in the decision-making processes.

As hard as it may be for you to believe, our church business conferences, under this **SALT & SPICE** arrangement, are usually very well-attended and they're like a breath of fresh air to our people. Almost always when I leave these gatherings, I think, *I really believe that the Lord has always intended for His people to conduct His business in a manner somewhat similar to this!*

Chapter Eight

Who Does What?

Up until now we've been considering some of the things that church leaders do: They teach and instruct, inspire to service, care for others, and govern. But now let's take a look from a different angle. Are these leaders primarily vocational or lay?

A biblical and historical survey will indicate that from their earliest beginnings Christians have held the view that the two ongoing church leaders presented in the New Testament are:

1) Pastors/elders/bishops, three titles that are used interchangeably
2) Deacons[1]

Interestingly enough, the biblical qualifications for those who are called to lead and model ministry in these two offices are almost identical.[2] Furthermore, in the third chapter of 1 Timothy, the author moves almost seamlessly from discussing the qualifications of a pastor/elder/ bishop (vv. 1–7) to mentioning the qualifications of a deacon (vv. 8–13). So the primary difference between the two is that the office of pastor/elder/bishop is more vocational, while the office of deacon is more for the lay person.[3]

As you may already know, in today's culture the elder system is almost always comprised mostly of laypersons, not vocational ministers, but this is not what the New Testament seems to be saying, particularly as the church began to mature.

I don't want to sound contentious, and I also am aware that sincere Christians may have differing interpretations of the Scripture and still find common ground in their belief that the Bible is completely trustworthy, but the argument stated above seems almost airtight to me. Therefore, I respectfully disagree with those who insist that the elder system of government, led primarily by laypersons, is preferable scripturally. Is there a third church office mentioned in the New Testament?

I believe the function of pastors/elders/bishops is fulfilled best through the vocational staff, remembering that they can extend their ministries through the three lay leadership groups discussed in chapters 4 and 5. And, of these three lay leadership groups, only the deacons are mentioned in the New Testament as a lay church office.

The model that I am proposing seems consistent with the biblical thrust of the two church offices mentioned in the New Testament:

1) Pastors/elders/bishops, who are primarily vocational ministers. Today's equivalent would be members of the PLT.
2) Deacons, who are primarily lay ministers. Today's equivalent would be the members of the DMT.

Aside from the fact that elders in the biblical sense should be primarily vocational ministers, let me point out six other significant areas in which the model presented in this book differs from most elder systems of church government commonly in place today.

ELDER SYSTEM	PROPOSED STRUCTURE
Comprised of 4-8 men	Comprised of 12 men and women
Appointed by the senior pastor	*Elected* by the entire congregation
Serve for life	Rotate every 3 years
Senior pastor has voting and often even veto privileges	None of the PLT members vote; they serve as consultants and spiritual advisors
Elders function as a board of directors (i.e. "ruling elders")[4]	Management Team functions as a board of directors
Elders are accountable under God to each other	Management Team members are accountable under God to the congregation

That being said, let's look at the role of bi-vocational ministers. I want to affirm them. The purpose of examining this topic is not to denigrate their work, because their calling and services are vital throughout the world. We value them and applaud them for all of the hard work they are doing and for the huge contribution they're making. We recognize that most bi-vocational ministers, however, would want to build their work to the point where they could be full-time.

But, for the typical church, the model that I have presented to you is a biblical structure that works well. It's also effective because it cultivates the laity for ministry, assigns authority with responsibility to spiritually mature and competent Christians, and streamlines decision making.

1. Refer to Gene A. Getz, *Elders and Leaders: God's Plan for Leading the Church,* Chicago: Moody Publishers, 2003, p. 27. Also refer to Appendix 1 of John Piper's *Biblical Eldership,* Desiring God Ministries, 1999, Minneapolis, Minnesota.
2. These qualifications are listed and defined in the Deacon Handbook and the Management Team Handbook, which are found in Appendix #1.
3. A similar phenomenon seems to occur in Acts 6 where the vocational ministers needed spiritually gifted laypersons to assist them in the ministry so they could spend more of their time in prayer and the study of God's Word.
4. As a matter of church history, Daniel L. Akin points out that the distinction between "teaching elders" and "ruling elders" doesn't appear until the time of John Calvin. Furthermore, this distinction hinges only on a very questionable interpretation of a single verse (1 Timothy 5:17). See p. 64 in chapter 1 of *Perspectives on Church Government: Five Views of Church Polity,* edited by Chad Owen Brown and R. Stanton Norman, Broadman and Holman Publishers, 2004.

Chapter Nine

Church Conflict

All of us wish that the church would be a picture of perfect harmony and that her image would never be tarnished, but we've seen so many cases where dysfunction is far too apparent. It just seems to happen and often catches us blindsided. The church's image is sullied, often with little or no restraints, people are wounded, and there's trouble all around.

Sadly, in many churches no medium exists for the church to work through these conflicts in a way that honors God. Instead, the leaders simply respond with a knee-jerk reaction in the heat of battle. This often heats things up even more, and is the key reason why there should be a plan—before it's needed—for properly resolving conflict if and when it shows up.

May I offer some biblical principles and some very practical and workable suggestions for resolving these typical church problems? When those inevitable disputes come up within the church, wisdom would dictate that the church not discuss them initially and fully at a church-wide meeting for all to hear. As you know, in such all-church gatherings, there are often people who are far from God; others may be visiting; new believers who are still spiritually immature might also be in attendance; and impressionable young people could be present too. In fact, I have often wondered how many young people have decided not to pursue a life of vocational ministry simply because of what they have seen occur in some church business meetings.

So the question is: How should disagreements within the church be resolved?

Thankfully, the answer may be found in a number of different passages of Scripture, but nowhere better than in Acts 15,[1] where we read that some godly leaders met together in a private session to seek a solution to a disagreement in the church (v. 6). The relevant application here is that the entire church was not involved initially in trying to resolve the dispute. Rather, Paul and Barnabas, the apostles, the elders, and James, who was the senior pastor of the church in Jerusalem, ironed out everything in a private meeting. Only then did they present the matter to the entire congregation at Jerusalem (v. 22) and eventually to the one at Antioch (vv. 30–35).

Let me point out that their final step in resolving their differences—presenting the matter to the whole church body—may not always be necessary, depending upon the nature of the problem. But their method of handling church conflict was consistent with Jesus' teaching as outlined in Matthew 18:15–17 where discernable steps are given: personal and private discussion, establishment of the case by two or three witnesses, and finally reporting to the church.

With these principles in mind, let me offer another practical suggestion regarding how disputes or misunderstandings may be resolved in churches today. In our congregation we make it clear that any member of our church can make an appointment to attend one of our weekly staff meetings to voice a concern. If the issue is one of the mind and not of the heart, then the question can usually be answered by one of the members of our PLT.[2]

Once it becomes common knowledge among the congregation that each church member has this type of access to the entire PLT, it has been my experience that very few people will even want to schedule such an appointment. The church members seem satisfied and content just knowing the ministerial staff can be approached openly and transparently on a weekly basis.

Hopefully, in such a venue, the problem can be resolved respectfully with a spirit of love and prayer. If not, then the next recourse would be for the individual to meet with our Conciliation Team from within the Deacon Ministry Team (DMT). If the matter cannot be settled at that level, it is then turned over to the MT.[3] Depending on the issue, the Conciliation Team and/or the MT may need to reference the Church Membership Covenant,[4] which is based solidly on Scripture, to remind the individual what he agreed to when he completed his Church Membership Orientation.

The MT is empowered, if necessary, to employ disciplinary action through a formal recommendation to the congregation.[5] One would think that disciplinary action might have a very divisive effect on the church, but, in a carefully researched essay, Greg Wills provides evidence to the contrary. Wills found that churches often experienced their greatest revival during those periods in which they practiced church discipline.[6] The gospel message has little power unless churches are distinct from the world, and church discipline is one of the ways that this distinction might, unfortunately, have to be made. Furthermore, when church discipline is implemented carefully and consistently, the purity and unity of the church can be better maintained.

In dealing with church conflict at each of these levels, the purpose would be to operate within the thrust of the actions taken by the Jerusalem Council (Acts 15) and according to Jesus' teaching as seen in Matthew 18:15–17.

1. In his book *An Introduction to the New Testament* (Anchor Bible Reference Library; New York: Doubleday, 1997), p. 306, Raymond E. Brown states that this convocation in Jerusalem was "the most important meeting ever held in the history of Christianity." Similarly, F.F. Bruce, in *The Book of Acts,* New International Commentary on the New Testament, rev. ed. (Grand Rapids: Eerdmans, 1988), p. 282, asserts that the Acts 15 assembly was "an event to which Luke attaches the highest importance; it is as epoch-making, in his eyes, as the conversion of Paul or the preaching of the gospel to Cornelius and his household."

2 Inviting them to attend such a meeting also encourages the individual to state the issue succinctly.

3. Disciplinary action can usually fall into one of three broad categories. First, and the least severe, would be a rebuke. Second, there could be a time of probation during which prayerful modeling and monitoring would occur. Finally, there could be expulsion.

4. See Section I.C.

5. See Section I.E.4.

6. "The Church: Baptists and Their Churches in the Eighteenth and Nineteenth Centuries," by Greg Wills, pp. 19-42, *Polity: Biblical Arguments on How to Conduct Church Life,* Edited by Mark Dever, Nine Marks Ministries, 2001.

Chapter Ten

How to Transition

When church affairs are handled with excellence, God is glorified and people are inspired. Isn't that what you want? With this in mind, let me share with you a number of steps to carefully and methodically take in order to help your church make this transition into excellence.

First, *the senior leadership must recognize a need to undergo such a change.* Do your present constitution and bylaws reflect biblical principles, or are they patterned after secular models? Do they help your members flourish and grow as Christ followers? Is there a plan for working through conflicts within the church? Are the spiritual, emotional and physical needs of the people being met? Is there accountability? Are these documents legal in the eyes of the government? All of these are issues that shouldn't be overlooked. This book can serve as a helpful tool in educating the senior leadership to all of these critical issues that need to be considered.

Second, *the church needs to appoint a task force to clarify its vision/mission and to recommend a biblical church structure.* You might call this a Church Mission and Structure Task Force. This should be a fairly large group—19 laypersons in our case—and should be comprised of men and women who are spiritually mature, have a visionary outlook, and demonstrate cooperative spirits. There are two tasks they'll need to work on.

- The first is to once again examine the Scriptures to understand more fully the vision/mission of the church and the biblical purposes of the church. For example, the vision statement of our church is "to develop people into fully devoted followers of Jesus Christ." We do this by following the five biblical purposes for the church (Acts 2:46–47)—worship, fellowship, discipleship, ministry, and outreach. If you're interested in using our document as a possible model, it can be found in Appendix #5. I recommend that you present your mission statement for adoption by the church several months before you present the constitution and bylaws so that your church's structure is designed to facilitate your vision.
- The second task they'll need to work on is church structure; i.e., the constitution and bylaws. This may take several months to accomplish. I would suggest that you eventually break the task force into subcommittees to work on individual sections of the constitution and bylaws. Later, when they come back together, each subcommittee can then lead a discussion of the section it worked on.

  You may want to use Mountain Park's constitution and bylaws plus those of several other churches as a starting point, always checking them against what you've now found to be true in Scripture. The Task Force at Mountain Park worked faithfully with our ministerial staff for eight months. They critically analyzed the material I brought from Grand Avenue, as well as that from other churches, and came up with an excellent document.

  Although some people doubted this many minds could ever reach a consensus (especially because many of the members had such strong personalities), that's exactly what happened. Our discussions and debates were sometimes blunt and forthright, yet this large group of competent, educated and often opinionated Christian men and women came to a unanimous decision about our proposed church structure. They persevered and it paid off. They ended up with an improved and absolutely wonderful model. So, if it takes a while and if there are some unexpected hurdles, don't become discouraged. Having it right can bring huge dividends and prevent unnecessary pain and sorrow later.

Third, *after much of the groundwork has been laid, the task force needs to get expert legal counsel.* I can't overstate the importance of this step. This is a dimension that's often overlooked and can bring public embarrassment, unnecessary expense, and ugly lawsuits if it is not done properly. In our setting, late in the process we brought in Mr. David Doverspike,[1] a committed Christian leader and an experienced attorney, whose areas of expertise include church and denominational litigation. He offered many extremely helpful suggestions, making certain that our constitution and bylaws conformed to Georgia corporate law. When we presented our proposed constitution and bylaws to our people, we asked him to be there to answer questions relating to legal matters. This was a wise decision because it helped our people more fully understand the necessity of this update. His expert opinion alleviated many of their concerns.

Those of you who choose to use our constitution and bylaws as a model can find a strong comfort level in being assured that they pass legal muster in Georgia, thus saving you the cost of some expensive legal fees which we paid at the front end of the process. Plus, engaging an attorney at this point will more than pay for itself when you are able to circumvent potential legal difficulties later.

Fourth, *a proper protocol needs to be established in presenting the recommendation of the task force to the congregation.* Here are some ideas.

- Distribute printed materials that provide background information addressing major questions and possible concerns before they are raised publicly.
- Conduct a series of town hall meetings, perhaps four to six in all, in order to accommodate busy schedules. Each meeting needs to be broken down into small interest groups according to each section of the constitution and bylaws. These smaller groups ought to be led by the subcommittee members (mentioned above) who worked on that section. This allows church members to go to the venue that deals with their specific concerns, provides people with an opportunity to ask their questions in a more private setting, and dilutes the public influence of that small but ever-present number of people who just like to complain.
- Be deliberate and thorough, never defensive. Keep in mind that the members of the congregation need time to digest lots of material, material that the members of the task force have been studying for months.
- Keep emphasizing that this new constitution and bylaws will free up the laity for effective and fulfilling ministry, is biblical, is legal, has adequate checks against abuse of authority, and presents a New Testament plan for conflict resolution. For a church that's seeking to pattern itself after God's

blueprint, the fact that it's biblical is the ultimate ace in the hole.

- Use this book as a resource for answering questions in a comprehensive manner. It'll be to your advantage.

***Finally,** at the time of your vote, remind the members of your congregation that there's only one perfect document in the world, and it certainly is not this constitution and bylaws!* So, in your desire to pursue the truth wherever it might lead and to improve everything in your church to glorify God more fully, ask your church members to live with their new structure for a year. During that time, scrutinize it to discover ways in which it might be improved. If you find any problems, fix them in a timely manner. When this reevaluation by the Management Team took place at Mountain Park, I'm happy to report that we didn't detect any major pitfalls.

Once this structure is adopted by your church, you'll have a biblical and useful instrument under which to operate more smoothly. This will then allow you to concentrate more on the true mission of your church.

1. You may also be interested to know that David Doverspike is the son of a prominent but now deceased pastor.

Chapter Eleven

What to Expect

We've just looked at important steps to follow when you transition a church from where it probably was to where it needs to be. Please don't skirt any of these steps. They're all important. You and the church leadership have committed your efforts to the Lord in prayer, worked hard, and presented it to the congregation. What kind of response can you now expect from them?

If you're in a church that's already been operating from a somewhat standard foundation, then you can usually expect to be faced with some challenges in your transition. Ideally, all the prep work you've done has helped your people recognize a need for change and made them enthusiastic about moving forward. Hopefully, there is enough trust among everyone so that, although it may be new, they will say, "Yes! We're willing to try it and move forward!"

The first time I led a church in this transition, they were ready for it. They had just experienced "those church sorrows and heartaches that ought not to be" and were ready for a better way. *They embraced a new biblical church structure almost without a hitch and all went well.* They had a beautiful spirit and I was a grateful pastor.

But there's no guarantee that every congregation will support this change. It may not be quite as easy as you had expected. The PLT and the Task Force may have had total unity and did everything they knew to do, but the response from the congregation may not be what you had hoped for. *The church might respond reluctantly,* and there may be several reasons for this.

- Blind loyalty to the tenets of the former constitution and bylaws may be a problem, especially if they were drawn up under the ministry of a former senior pastor who had a very long tenure of leadership. It's likely that some within this group may even be largely uninformed about the particulars of the old structure. They probably haven't studied the documents with a biblical frame of reference and so they don't recognize the pitfalls.
- They may be tradition-driven and are heavily influenced by the way they've always done things in the past. The new structure, however biblical, represents something they have never done before and so they're quite skeptical.
- They are simply opposed to change.
- They are following a vocal and influential few who are reluctant to embrace it.
- They may not have even read the new document and are uninformed about its merits, but they just don't like it. Yes, this really happens!

How do you manage the challenges that a vocal minority can pose? I would suggest that you simply remind the church repeatedly that this proposed structure is well-grounded within the thrust of Scripture; it helps the members flourish in ministry and grow as Christ followers; it incorporates a plan for working through conflict within the church; it helps meet the spiritual, emotional and physical needs of the people; there's more than adequate accountability; and it's legal in the eyes of the law. Yes, not all of the terms used in the new constitution and bylaws will be familiar to the members, but all can learn and grow. Everyone will adjust to these terms eventually since all of the concepts are biblical.

But now the question is: "What should the leadership do if a *majority of the congregation totally resists these changes?*" It's hard for me to imagine that occurring, especially if all five steps described in the previous chapter have been followed, but it is possible. Under such dire circumstances, it's probably best simply to acquiesce to their concerns and stay with the old structure for the foreseeable future. It's not worth splitting the church. The pastor could lovingly state something to the effect that, "Even in the middle of a less than good decision by the majority of our membership (to reject the new church structure), I will remain as your pastor and help us all work together as best we can." But once you've seen the light, it's difficult to function with a church structure that is in desperate need of revision.

If you're a church planter, or a missionary, and starting from scratch, then you're at a strong advantage. *You won't need to go through a transition; you can do it biblically, right from the beginning and then build on a strong foundation.*

Who wouldn't want all the good that can come from a healthy church? Are you willing to try turning dysfunction to health? Thankfully, you now have something in print to help you structure your church based on a biblical model.

Chapter Twelve

Leading Well

It's almost impossible to find a great biblical scholar who has had experience in effectively leading an organization or business. It took me a long time to discover that these two areas of giftedness—teaching and leading—are almost always mutually exclusive, but upon further reflection it makes sense. True scholars need to be experts in their field of study, and that can become an all-consuming pursuit, leaving little time to lead anything else well. True leaders, on the other hand, are so busy leading well that they don't have time to devote most of their attention to any one particular area of study. This reality is the cause for the perpetual tension that is felt on the campuses of our seminaries. Is the primary purpose of a seminary education to produce vocational ministers who are good teachers or good leaders?

Most university and seminary professors, out of sheer necessity, have never had an opportunity to successfully lead an organization or business. The result is that by the time most seminarians graduate, they have been carefully taught the Scriptures but have not been properly taught how to lead effectively. In turn, when these pastoral graduates begin to serve in local congregations, those congregants are well-taught, hopefully, but not always properly led. This certainly was true in my case, and I know it's true in the cases of almost every pastor I've known. Perhaps this is one of the primary reasons why there are almost no publications dealing with how to lead a church properly based on a biblical church structure.

When my wife and I finished the grind of a decade of seminary study, I believed that the only three components for an effective ministry were to love the Lord, His Word, and people. Obviously, all three of those components are essential and even non-negotiable, but something more is needed because it takes more than just sincerity and love and dedication for a church to make a vital impact on the world; it also takes leadership. In fact, the future viability of the church depends on the quality of leadership we exercise today.

This is why I want to challenge you to see if you might have within you the untapped gift of leadership. As you do so, let me challenge you to improve your leadership skills by reading everything you can on this topic as your time and budget allow. Furthermore, attend seminars and conferences where leadership is taught. Try to interact as much as possible with someone who is ahead of you in leadership; let them mentor you. And, if you want to improve your leadership skills, then you have to actually lead someone or something. It's at this point that I want to close this book by tightening our focus. I want to challenge you to ask the Lord to help you lead your church properly—not just to teach well, but also to lead well. One of your leadership goals should be to structure the church in which you are serving according to the principles found in the Scriptures. If you do this, then God will help you lead your church members to maximize ministry and minimize maintenance by reducing the number of unnecessary meetings that drain the time and energy of your people.

I'm familiar with those passages of Scripture that teach that, strictly speaking, everything we do is an act of worship. But still there's that variable called "discretionary time." Poor use of discretionary time can get our people so involved in unnecessary church meetings that they have very little time left over to impact those within their respective circles of influence who are far from God. This is why a biblical church structure is so important. It streamlines our efforts. I'm convinced that God wants the discretionary time of His people spent more on impacting others with the gospel than in unnecessary meetings where we beat the same old horses to death!

As you know, in the military, in the heat of battle the real teamwork and harmony happen on the front lines. There's a great need for camaraderie when people are fighting together with a common purpose in a life-and-death battle. Go back five to ten miles from the front lines, however. That's where you'll find people complaining about the incidentals of life: the weather, the food, the lack of certain supplies, etc. With this in mind, it appears to me that our church structures are often conducive to wasting the valuable discretionary time of our people in activities that are miles away from the front lines, back where negativity and complaining can be fostered easily.

For your church to be on the front lines, making a significant impact for Christ upon the world, you must have three things.

- First, you must have a vision from the Lord of how to proceed, and you must then apply that vision to every area of your church's life. You must be purpose-driven.
- Second, you must have a biblical strategy of how to take people, no matter where they are in life, and develop them into fully devoted Christ followers who can reproduce themselves spiritually in the lives of others. You must have a plan for discipleship.
- Third, you must have an underlying biblical structure that will hold the whole thing together. In fact, almost every change you bring to your church will only be temporary and cosmetic until you deal with the basic framework; your underlying structure (constitution and bylaws) will eventually determine your entire philosophy of ministry. So I would challenge you to lead properly in this area.

God wants His people to point others to the Hope of the world. But it's almost impossible for a dysfunctional church to do a good job of this. Dysfunction creates fodder for the rumor mill; it causes our image to be blemished; we wound our own people; we become a mockery in the community rather than a magnet; and we just don't count for much spiritually. Ultimately the stakes are high because eternity is hanging in the balance for so many people, all of whom are very important to God.

Dysfunction doesn't have to be, however. We can do something about it. We can implement a biblical church structure that can lead to fitness. It will help us demonstrate joy in service, harmony, unity, care of our own and of others, and wise and responsible governance. We can serve as an excellent model of health. And it's a healthy church that can best lead others to the Hope of the world.

Appendix #1

FOUR HANDBOOKS

DEACON MINISTRY TEAM HANDBOOK

Mountain Park First Baptist Church

5485 Five Forks Trickum Road
Stone Mountain, GA 30087-3045
Phone: 770.921.1452 www.mpfbc.org

Our vision is to develop people into fully devoted followers of Jesus Christ

TABLE OF CONTENTS

Mountain Park First Baptist Church

5485 FIVE FORKS TRICKUM ROAD • STONE MOUNTAIN, GA 30087
770-921-1452 • FAX 770-564-9526
Web Site www.mpfbc.org

DR. BILL BLANCHARD, SENIOR PASTOR

Dear Nominee,

Before you can answer the question "Do I want to become a deacon?" you must first ask yourself "Why do I want to become a deacon?" Do you want to be a leader of the church or a servant to the church? Traditionally, many churches have defined the deacon body as "managers" over the church; however, Jesus Christ plainly expresses His desire for the leaders and deacons to be primarily spiritual mentors and servants *to* the church and not just managers *over* the church.

Jesus instructed his disciples that, ". . . whoever desires to become great among you, let him be your servant . . . just as the Son of Man did not come to be served, but to serve. . . ." Matthew 20:26-28 (NKJV)

Acts 6:1-6 describes a potentially divisive issue that confronted the early church. The issue was resolved when deacons were chosen to serve fairly the needs of the widows of the church and to free the apostles to devote themselves to prayer and to the ministry of the Word of God.

As the Deacon Ministry Team seeks to serve Christ and His church, it will play a key role in fulfilling the vision of the Mountain Park First Baptist Church to develop people into fully devoted followers of Jesus Christ.

The following handbook is designed to give you the qualifications of a deacon, as well as to provide an overview to the commitments and functions of the deacon-led ministry teams. As you review this material, please take time to be certain that you sense the calling of Jesus Christ to lead the church by being a servant *to* His people.

Your Servants in Jesus' Name,

The Nominating Committee
Mountain Park First Baptist Church

Deacon Ministry Team Responsibilities

The Deacon Ministry Team of the Mountain Park First Baptist Church shall assume the following responsibilities:

1) The deacon shall be an example of service and ministry by leading and serving on one or more of the deacon-led ministry teams.

2) The Deacon Ministry Team shall lead the congregation in its observances of the Lord's Supper.

3) The Deacon Ministry Team shall be prepared to assist the Senior Pastor at all worship services in receiving new members. This includes being able to walk someone through the plan of salvation.

4) The Deacon Ministry Team shall serve as a council of advice and as a prayer partner to the Senior Pastor and other members of the Pastoral Leadership Team.

5) The Deacon Ministry Team and their wives shall maintain a prayer chain ministry.

6) The Deacon Ministry Team shall oversee the benevolent ministry of the Church, investigating and providing assistance to those in need. They will determine when and how much financial support should be provided by the Church on a short-term basis.

7) The Deacon Ministry Team shall assign one deacon each Sunday to serve as Deacon of the Week. The Deacon of the Week shall have the following responsibilities:
   - He shall lead the Sunday morning pre-service prayer time in the church parlor.
   - He shall lead the offertory prayer during the Sunday morning worship service(s).
   - He and his wife shall prepare the visitor reception in the church parlor and assist the Senior Pastor and his wife in greeting guests.
   - He shall pick up the visitor cards from the usher room on Sunday morning and Sunday evening and contact visitors as soon as possible during the assigned week.
   - He shall follow up with visits to visitors as needed and match the needs of the visitor with the appropriate Sunday School or other organization in the Church.

8) The deacon shall serve for a term of three (3) years (unless filling an unexpired term).

9) The deacon shall be fully supportive of all deacons' meetings and other deacon-sponsored events in the Church.

10) The deacon, as a spiritual leader, shall be a model by setting the standard for interaction and fellowship with others by greeting people in the lobby and worship center before and after each service. He shall be especially sensitive to introduce himself to visitors and those members with whom he is unfamiliar.

Biblical Requirements of a Deacon

The primary purpose of every deacon should be to serve "The Body of Christ" in accordance with the intention and practice of this ministry in the New Testament. Models for deacon service are found in the following passages.

Acts 6:1-6 (NJKV) records that:

> "Now in those days, when the number of the disciples was multiplying, there arose a complaint against the Hebrews by the Hellenists, because their widows were neglected in the daily distribution. Then the twelve summoned the multitude of the disciples and said, "It is not desirable that we should leave the word of God and serve tables. Therefore, brethren, seek out from among you seven men of good reputation, full of the Holy Spirit and wisdom, whom we may appoint over this business; but we will give ourselves continually to prayer and to the ministry of the word." And the saying pleased the whole multitude. And they chose Stephen, a man full of faith and the Holy Spirit, and Philip, Prochorus, Nicanor, Timon, Parmenas, and Nicolas, a proselyte from Antioch, whom they set before the apostles; and when they had prayed, they laid hands on them."

In I Timothy 3:8-13 (NKJV), Paul gives the following instructions:

> "Likewise deacons must be reverent, not double-tongued, not given to much wine, not greedy for money, holding the mystery of the faith with a pure conscience. But let these also first be tested; then let them serve as deacons, being found blameless. Likewise, their wives must be reverent, not slanderers, temperate, faithful in all things. Let deacons be the husbands of one wife, ruling their children and their own houses well. For those who have served well as deacons obtain for themselves a good standing and great boldness in the faith which is in Christ Jesus."

A closer examination of these two passages reveals that a deacon should meet the following qualifications:

1) "Good reputation" (Acts 6:3) — A deacon's integrity must be beyond reproach in the Church as well as in daily conduct so as to inspire respect and confidence in the Gospel. His Christian witness should be reinforced by his trustworthy character.

2) "Full of the Holy Spirit" (Acts 6:3) — A deacon's life is daily permeated with the Spirit of God who brings holiness to his life and power to do through him what he cannot do on his own.

3) "Wisdom" (Acts 6:3) — A deacon should be wise enough to control his temper and disposition. Furthermore, wisdom must be attained as deacons immerse themselves in the Word of God so that God might pour out His mind in them.

4) "Full of faith" (Acts 6:5) — A deacon needs to have an immovable faith in God that will dare to lead the Church forward in the work of the Kingdom, in spite of obstacles that may dishearten many others.

5) "Reverent" (I Tim. 3:8) — A deacon must be firm in his faith, stable in his convictions, sound in his beliefs, and correct in his Church loyalty. This word "reverent" signifies weight. In this sense, it speaks of one who carries weight, or one who counts for right influences.

6) "Not double-tongued" (I Tim. 3:8) — A deacon's word should be truthful and sincere. A deacon is a man of his word and consistent in his speech. He never gives rise to misunderstandings and differences.

7) "Not given to much wine" (I Tim. 3:8) — A deacon, in his role as a spiritual mentor, should abstain from a beverage which has the ability to intoxicate.

8) "Not greedy for money" (I Tim. 3:8) — A deacon must not be covetous in the manner in which he earns, spends, and saves his money, in his management of Church funds, or in bringing his tithes and offerings to his local Church.

9) "Holding the mystery of the faith with a pure conscience" (I Tim. 3:9) — A deacon should be sound and stable in the teachings of the Bible and genuinely committed to believing and living out the revealed truths of the Christian faith.

10) "First be tested . . . being found blameless" (I Tim. 3:10) — A deacon should not be a new convert, but tested and proven to be a growing and maturing Christian who is above reproach and fully devoted to God.

11) "Husbands of one wife" (I Tim. 3:12) — A deacon is to be totally devoted to his wife, maintaining singular devotion, affection, and sexual purity in both thought and deed. The biblical exception that would allow for a Christian to divorce his spouse is sexual immorality (marital unfaithfulness) on the part of his spouse (Matthew 19:9). The Bible also takes into account the life of a deacon's wife in determining his qualifications to serve (Matthew 5:32; I Corinthians 7:10-11). Therefore, a man married to a divorced woman should not serve as a deacon unless the grounds for her divorce meet the biblical exception of sexual immorality (marital unfaithfulness) on the part of her former spouse. Under no circumstances should a divorce prior to a man or woman's conversion experience necessarily prohibit a deacon from service (II Corinthians 5:17; Ephesians 1:7). The Bible also teaches that under certain circumstances it is better for a man not to marry. Therefore, an unmarried man may serve as a deacon (Matthew 19:11-12).

12) "Ruling their children and their own houses well" (I Tim. 3:12) — A deacon should manage his home and exercise control over his children to the best of his ability. He should be respected as the spiritual head of his household.

Other Requirements of a Deacon

Beyond these biblical requirements, the Deacon Ministry Team of the Mountain Park First Baptist Church believes that our Lord Jesus, and every member of this church, may expect each deacon, as a spiritual leader, to serve as a model in the following areas:

1) He should support the Senior Pastor and other members of the Pastoral Leadership Team by freeing them to serve in accordance with their calling.

2) He should support all phases of the Church programs to the best of his ability with his attendance, gifts, talents, prayers and substance.

3) He should be a faithful and systematic tither in accordance with Scripture, knowing that the tithe is a minimum requirement. He should pledge to give at least one-tenth of his total income to the support of Mountain Park First Baptist Church.

4) He should be evangelistic and missionary in spirit, deeply interested in the salvation of people at home and abroad (see the example of Philip in Acts 8).

5) He should agree to act and speak in Christian love. He should be fully cooperative with his Senior Pastor, Pastoral Leadership Team, and Church. He should be able to refrain from destructive criticism, willing to settle all differences in a quiet and Christian manner.

6) He should keep in secrecy those things that should not be discussed with others, especially sensitive proceedings from all deacons' meetings.

7) He should zealously guard the spirit of unity within the Church.

8) He should further strive for unity within the deacon body. For example, once a decision has been made at a deacons' meeting, regardless of how much internal discussion and debate transpire among the deacon body, he should emerge in one accord.

9) He should, as a spiritual leader, understand his position to be one of "ministering servant." The wishes of the congregation must have priority over his personal wishes. He must be devoted to the spiritual welfare of the Church.

10) He should accept the "Baptist Faith and Message (2000)" as a doctrinal statement of his Christian beliefs.

Qualifications of a Deacon's Wife

If a deacon is married, the Bible also provides some qualifications for his wife. These, too, need to be weighed in the life of a man who is considered for the ministry of a deacon. They are as follows (I Timothy 3:11, NKJV):

1) "Reverent" — The wife of a deacon should have a sincere Christian purpose, with a great reverence for spiritual matters. For the fuller meaning of this word, see "reverent" as applied to the deacons (page 4 of this handbook).

2) "Not slanderers" — The wife of a deacon should not be known to give a false report concerning someone else.

3) "Temperate" — The wife of a deacon should be well-balanced spiritually, and calm in her dealings with others.

4) "Faithful in all things" — The wife of a deacon must be an exemplary member of the church to which her family belongs. Furthermore, she must be loyal and fully supportive to her husband. Others should see in her a heart of faithfulness in the Kingdom of God, in spite of obstacles that may dishearten many others.

Deacon Ministry Team Overview

There are five primary functions of the Deacon Ministry Team at the Mountain Park First Baptist Church:

1) Resolve conflicts
2) Serve the physical, emotional, and spiritual needs of people
3) Relieve the Senior Pastor and Pastoral Leadership Team so that they may offer more attention "to prayer and to the ministry of the Word of God"
4) Provide internal accountability
5) Assist the deacon officers in coordinating pulpit supply and interim pastorate on an as needed basis

You will note that the deacons do not function as the "business managers" of the church because those responsibilities are assigned to the Management Team. This enables our deacons to be free for ministry to people.

We also believe that deacons are primarily spiritual mentors and not just spiritual managers. As such, every deacon is assigned leadership roles to see that the primary functions mentioned above are fulfilled. The organizational chart on the following page provides a synopsis of our various deacon-led ministry teams. All of these will be led by current members of our Deacon Ministry Team, and most of them will require our deacons to work closely with our Pastoral Leadership Team and Equipping Ministry Team to enlist, train, and organize many other Church members (according to their **S**piritual gifts, **H**eart, **A**bilities, **P**ersonality, **E**xperience) for effective ministry on these deacon-led ministry teams. Each of these teams will provide a report at our regularly scheduled deacons' meetings.

Finally, as the spiritual mentors and servants of our Church, our deacons need to set the example for others in their regular attendance at worship service and Bible study events, ministry, and our evangelistic and missionary efforts in our community and around the world.

Deacon Ministry Team Organizational Chart

Mountain Park First Baptist Church

5485 Five Forks Trickum Road, Stone Mountain, GA 30087

Conciliation Team	Caring Ministry Teams	Pastoral Ministry Teams	Deacon Accountability Team
	Benevolence Prayer Support Groups	Altar Workers Bereavement Communion Preparation Evangelism/Outreach Fellowship Financial Counseling GA Baptist Children's Home Helping Hands Homebound Hospital New Member Follow-Up Nursing Home Small Group Study Visitation/Outreach Welcome Widow	(Officers & Senior Pastor)

PS P:\Share\XP\bills book\DMT Handbook 1-29-07.wpd

EQUIPPING MINISTRY TEAM HANDBOOK

Mountain Park First Baptist Church
5485 Five Forks Trickum Road
Stone Mountain, GA 30087-3045
Phone: 770.921.1452www.mpfbc.org

Our vision is to develop people into fully devoted followers of Jesus Christ

Table of Contents

5485 Five Forks Trickum Road • Stone Mountain, GA 30087
770-921-1452 • FAX 770-564-9526
www.mpfbc.org

DR. BILL BLANCHARD, SENIOR PASTOR

Dear Nominee,

One of the most exciting and fulfilling things that a Christian can experience is to become involved in an effective ministry to others in the name of the Lord Jesus Christ, and it is the responsibility of those who serve on the Equipping Ministry Team to help see that this happens throughout our Church. How? By getting our people involved in various church ministry teams according to the SHAPE (Spiritual gifts, Heart/Passion, Abilities, Personality, Experiences) which God has given them.

As you may know, spiritual maturity is achieved in a variety of ways, but assuming that there are no health issues involved, ministry involvement is crucial to the development of one's spiritual maturity. We believe that the Equipping Ministry Team is the medium that God desires to use in our Church to unleash every member to follow his or her passion to serve the Lord in ministry.

You are being asked by the Nominating Committee to prayerfully consider service on the Equipping Ministry Team. Please read the following material to see if you have an interest in service, and then see if you meet the qualifications. In the near future, you will be contacted by a member of the Nominating Committee to schedule an appointment to discuss this further.

Your servants in Jesus' name,

The Nominating Committee
Mountain Park First Baptist Church

Composition, Qualifications, and Responsibilities

Composition

The Equipping Ministry Team (EMT) is composed of nine members of the Church at-large. Three members are elected annually to serve three-year terms. The Discipleship Pastor is the Pastoral Leadership Team (PLT) representative for the team.

Qualifications

Members of the EMT shall be exemplary in their conduct, discreet in judgment, of honest report, full of faith, and conscious that they shall set worthy examples of cooperation, love and loyalty for all members of the Church. They should be faithful at all Sunday services, unless hindered by reason of good conscience, so they are aware of the faithfulness of those they consider for positions. They must also be able to keep in secrecy those things discussed about members as they are considered and evaluated for leadership.

Responsibilities

It is the task of the EMT to identify, recruit, equip, lead, and deploy others to be involved in various ministries of the Church, with no time placed on their involvement. They will maintain a Ministry Discovery Notebook that will inform new members of the opportunities for ministry within our Church

Another responsibility of the EMT is to look for new ministries in which our Church needs to be involved, and recruit people for them. If someone feels led to begin a new ministry, the EMT will provide a Ministry Action Plan Packet to help turn it into a successful ministry.

On an annual basis the EMT will choose a Team Leader for each ministry. This leader will be responsible for planning, budgeting if needed, and recruitment. He/she will also be the primary contact through whom the PLT representative will work.

Other Requirements

Because ministry is rendered in the name of Jesus Christ and our Church, the highest spiritual character of its servants is a must. The character of the servants will never rise higher than those who enlist them. Therefore, we expect each member of the EMT to serve as a model in the following areas by:

- Being a faithful and systematic tither, knowing that the tithe is the minimum requirement that should be brought to the local storehouse (church) for the Lord's work.

- Being evangelistic and missionary in spirit, deeply interested in the salvation of people at home and abroad (see Acts 8).

- Being fully cooperative with the Senior Pastor, PLT, and the Church.

- Being able to refrain from destructive criticism, willing to settle all differences in a quiet and Christian manner.

- Striving for unity among members of the EMT. For example, once a decision has been made at a team meeting, regardless of how much internal debate and discussion transpire, they should emerge in one accord.

- Being a model of spiritual leadership by setting the standard for interaction and fellowship with others by greeting people in the lobby and worship center before and after each service. They should be especially sensitive to introduce themselves to visitors and those members with whom they are unfamiliar.

MANAGEMENT TEAM HANDBOOK

MOUNTAIN PARK
LIVE ON PURPOSE
LEAVE A LEGACY
FIRST BAPTIST CHURCH

Mountain Park First Baptist Church
5485 Five Forks Trickum Road
Stone Mountain, GA 30087-3045
Phone: 770.921.1452
www.mpfbc.org

Our vision is to develop people into fully devoted followers of Jesus Christ

Table of Contents

Mountain Park First Baptist Church

5485 FIVE FORKS TRICKUM ROAD • STONE MOUNTAIN, GA 30087
770-921-1452 • FAX 770-564-9526
Web Site www.mpfbc.org

DR. BILL BLANCHARD, SENIOR PASTOR

Dear Nominee:

There is ample evidence in the New Testament to show that the words elder/presbyter, shepherd/pastor, and bishop/overseer refer to the same person or office (see, for example, Acts 20:17, 28; I Peter 5:1-5). These titles refer to three different tasks or functions expected of the same person or church office.

God has called some to the full-time gospel ministry. In our church, we call these vocational servant-leaders our Pastoral Leadership Team, and they are called to serve in accordance with the functions described in the scriptures mentioned above and elsewhere. In addition to fulfilling these tasks themselves, the members of our Pastoral Leadership Team are also to equip three different lay leadership groups within our church to concentrate their efforts according to these functions, one of which is the Management Team. These lay leaders are to exercise oversight in the management and governance of the Church.

This handbook is designed to provide the qualifications of a Management Team member. As you review this material, please try to be certain that you sense the calling of the Lord Jesus Christ and feel that you meet the qualifications to lead our Church by being a servant to His people in the management and governance of our congregation.

Your servants in Jesus' name,

The Nominating Committee
Mountain Park First Baptist Church

An Overview of the Ministry of the Management Team

This overview is drawn from the Constitution and Bylaws of Mountain Park First Baptist Church, Inc., of Stone Mountain, Georgia (hereafter "MPFBC"), as it pertains to the Management Team (hereafter "MT"). It is not intended, however, to replace the specific language of the Constitution approved by the Church.

- The members of the MT are elected by the Church from the membership of MPFBC and are expected to meet the biblical qualifications included in this handbook. MT members are normally expected to serve three calendar-year terms on a staggered basis and cannot succeed themselves in office for two years.

- The MT consists of 12 members. The Senior Pastor and the Pastoral Leadership Team (hereafter "PLT") shall function on the MT in advisory roles as resource persons and are not eligible to vote. The MT elects officers from among its members on a calendar-year basis.

- The principle responsibilities of the MT are to provide accountability for the Senior Pastor, ensure the financial integrity of the Church, develop and adopt policies relating to the operation of the Church, supervise personnel matters of the Church, and, as the Board of Directors, handle all corporate affairs and business matters involving the Church.

- In the area of accountability for the Senior Pastor, the MT provides advice and counsel in planning, budgeting, staffing, coordinating, and implementing the various ministries of the Church.

- The MT provides an annual job performance review of the Senior Pastor, and the MT, only, can make a recommendation to the Church regarding the dismissal of the Senior Pastor.

- The MT recommends the annual budget to the Church, including a recommendation of annual salary and benefits for the entire Church staff. The MT is responsible for maintaining the integrity of all the financial activities of the Church. These specific duties are further defined in Section VI of the Constitution and By-Laws.

- The MT authorizes policies and procedures as are necessary to ensure that the Church can function effectively.

- The MT meets monthly, or more frequently, as necessary, depending on circumstances and special needs.

The MT has three standing subcommittees comprised of members of the MT:

- Finance subcommittee: This subcommittee reports to the MT on matters of finance, including preparation of a budget proposal.

- Policy and Legal Issues subcommittee: This subcommittee handles all legal issues and develops all policies and procedures that may arise or be brought to the MT's attention.

- Personnel subcommittee: This subcommittee handles matters relating to staffing—recommending salary, benefits, and other personnel issues.

These subcommittees meet as necessary, although the Finance subcommittee usually meets the same day prior to the regularly scheduled MT meeting.

Other subcommittees may also be formed from time to time. Occasionally, the MT may recommend the formation of an *ad hoc* committee or special task force using Church members. In these cases, the MT will recommend that the Nominating Committee appoint such a committee. Once appointed, these subcommittees function under the direction of and are accountable to the MT.

Biblical Requirements

The primary purpose of every MT member should be to serve "the body of Christ" in accordance with the intention and practice of this ministry in the New Testament, models of which are found in I Timothy 3:1-7 and Titus 1:5-9, shown below in the New King James translation.

I Tim. 3:1-7
This is a faithful saying: If a man desires the position of a bishop, he desires a good work. A bishop then must be blameless, the husband of one wife, temperate, sober-minded, of good behavior, hospitable, able to teach; not given to wine, not violent, not greedy for money, but gentle, not quarrelsome, not covetous; one who rules his own house well, having his children in submission with all reverence (for if a man does not know how to rule his own house, how will he take care of the church of God?); not a novice, lest being puffed up with pride he fall into the same condemnation as the devil. Moreover he must have a good testimony among those who are outside, lest he fall into reproach and the snare of the devil.

Titus 1:5-9
For this reason I left you in Crete, that you should set in order the things that are lacking, and appoint elders in every city as I commanded you–if a man is blameless, the husband of one wife, having faithful children not accused of dissipation or insubordination. For a bishop must be blameless, as a steward of God, not self-willed, not quick-tempered, not given to wine, not violent, not greedy for money, but hospitable, a lover of what is good, sober-minded, just, holy, self-controlled, holding fast the faithful word as he has been taught, that he may be able, by sound doctrine, both to exhort and convict those who contradict.

As we look at these two passages, we see that the following Scriptural standards should be exemplified in the lives of those who are on the MT:

1. **"Blameless"** (Timothy); **"blameless as a steward of God"** (Titus)
   A MT member must not be vulnerable to attack on the grounds of moral or doctrinal issues. Members of the Church and community should be able to point to a MT member as an example of one who fulfills the duties of a Christian and supports the mission and vision of his/her Church.

2. **"Husband of one wife"** (Timothy & Titus)
   When our Church adopted a new Constitution and Bylaws (May 21, 2006), it was decided that the primary ones to take the initiative in managing, governing, leading, and directing the affairs of our Church would be the members of our MT. As such, these members would fulfill the lay duties of the overseer/bishop whose qualifications are listed in I Timothy 3:1-7 and Titus 1:5-9. During the time of transition to this new structure, the members of the Finance Committee, Personnel Committee, and Trustees were the initial ones who comprised our MT. Since there is neither male or female in Christ Jesus (Galatians 3:28), and because

there are examples of women serving in managing, governing, leading, and directing roles in both the Old and New Testaments, and since it has always been the practice of MPFBC to have men and women serving on these entities as listed above, the Church chose to continue this practice with the members of the MT. It is within this context that we interpret the thrust of this biblical requirement as being concerned primarily with the fact that a member of the MT should be faithful, loving, and loyal to his/her spouse. As such, he/she should also be a model of sexual purity with his/her spouse.

3. **"Temperate"** (Timothy)
A temperate person is one who keeps careful watch on his/her conduct, guarding against sin in any form. For this reason, a MT member must be aware of his/her strengths and weaknesses. This balanced, or tempered, view of himself/herself makes him/her more qualified to take a rational, composed view of the affairs of the Church.

4. **"Sober-minded"** (Timothy & Titus)
Building on a temperate view of themselves and the affairs of the Church, a sober-minded person will have a solid understanding of the issues when participating in decision-making. They will be persons of learning, seeking to gain knowledge and understanding, so that they will not make hasty judgments. This attitude of learning will lead them to ask probing questions and make dispassionate decisions, further enhancing their effectiveness in office.

5. **"Of good behavior"** (Timothy)
Just as he/she is to be blameless, a MT member should communicate order, decency, and correctness in his/her appearance, conduct, and speech. A person of sober mind (internal behavior) will also be a person of sober conduct (external behavior).

6. **"Hospitable"** (Timothy & Titus)
A hospitable MT member is, literally, a "lover of strangers," ready to receive others into his/her home, and give aid to those who need it.

7. **"Able to teach"** (Timothy)/**"holding fast the faithful word"** (Titus)/**"able, by sound doctrine, both to exhort and convict those who contradict"** (Titus)
A member of the MT should not only be wise, but should also be ready and able to communicate such wisdom to others through responsible instruction. The ability to teach, however, is not enough. Because all effective leaders are learners, a MT member must first of all be a learner himself/herself, so that he/she is able to teach from the overflow of his/her own studies, and those studies must be founded on the Bible (i.e., "the faithful word" and "sound doctrine"). The wisdom of a MT member allows him/her to be completely transparent before others, including his/her fellow team members. Thus he/she has no hidden agenda behind his/her comments or questions, which frees the entire team to participate in Spirit-led decision making.

8. **"Not given to wine"** (Timothy & Titus)
When this phrase is considered in light of the more complete revelation of God as recorded in all of Scripture, the interpretation which the MT subscribes to is as follows: Especially in their role as spiritual mentors, it is our belief that the Lord intends for MT members to abstain from a beverage which has the ability to intoxicate.

9. **"Not violent"** (Timothy & Titus)/**"Not quarrelsome"** (Timothy)
MT members are to be peaceable, and not those whose personality traits lead them to be quarrelsome, disruptive, or divisive. They are physically and emotionally able to control their reaction to other people or ideas, enabling them to employ good conflict resolution skills. In church governance, disputes will occasionally arise, and a MT member must be ready to deal with those situations gently but directly. Once again, we see "temperance" and "sober-mindedness" dictating outward behavior, ensuring that all things by the MT are done in good order.

10. **"Not greedy for money"** (Timothy & Titus)/**"As a steward of God"** (Titus)/**"Not covetous"** (Timothy)
MT members must not be covetous or greedy in the manner in which they earn, spend, and save their money, in the management of church funds, or in bringing their tithes and offerings to their local Church.

11. **"Gentle"** (Timothy)
MT members are to display a kind demeanor. They are to be patient and willing to learn from others, not presuming that they have the answer to all questions or situations. They are meek in their dependence on the wisdom of God, and open to all sources of godly insight.

12. **"One who rules their own house well, having his children in submission with all reverence"** (Timothy)/**"having faithful children"** (Titus)
MT members should manage their home and exercise control over their children to the best of their ability. As a spiritual leader of the Church, and because they are a key role model to other Church members, a MT member must fulfill this requirement in his/her private life.

13. **"Not a novice"** (Timothy)
MT members should not be a new convert, but tested and proven to be a mature, growing Christian. The Greek word literally means, "one newly planted." Just as a new plant may have difficulty standing up to a storm, a new Christian may lack the life experience that enables him/her to persevere in difficult situations. Leadership is often a key ability exhibited by those who are "not novices," and qualified MT members are no exceptions. As a tested, growing Christian, a MT member will be able to provide leadership as he/she draws on his/her biblical maturity as well as the discernment and wisdom God provides.

14. **"A good testimony among those who are outside"** (Timothy)
The standing of a MT member in the non-Christian community ("those outside") should be beyond reproach, even by those whose moral values may fall far short of the biblical ideal. The misguided view of non-Christians that the church is a place of hypocrisy must never be based on the conduct of a MT member.

15. **"Not self-willed"** (Titus)
A self-willed MT member would be determined to have his/her own way in every matter, which would lead to disruption and divisiveness. Just as a temperate person is aware of his/her strengths and weaknesses, a MT member must not set his/her own judgment as superior to all others. He/she will instead take a balanced approach to decision-making and avoid always taking the lead in discussions or debates. This flexible approach to decision-

making means a MT member also has the ability to reconsider decisions in light of new facts or evidence that might suggest a different course of action. A self-willed MT member might find it difficult to yield to new styles or methods when those are in conflict with his/her personal preferences.

16. **"Not quick tempered"** (Titus)
When disagreements occur, the MT members must exercise self-control. The Bible does not prohibit anger, but it does prohibit the inappropriate expression of anger. A MT member must be a model in this regard, both in public exchanges and in private meetings.

17. **"A lover of what is good"** (Titus)
Love seeks what is best for another, whether it be an individual or the Church as a whole. In fulfilling his/her responsibility, a MT member will seek to embrace the best, for the good of the Church. This requires a MT member to maintain a broad perspective of the overall needs of the Church by seeking the best course of action when many good options exist. This also means that an individual MT member may have to defer to the collective wisdom of the entire MT when unanimity does not occur on a particular issue.

18. **"Just"** (Titus)
A just MT member will exhibit integrity in dealings with all people. He/she will seek justice in each situation, desiring the best for the Church as a whole.

19. **"Holy"** (Titus)
God calls Christians "a chosen people, a royal priesthood, a holy nation" (I Peter 2:9). As such, we are sanctified, or set apart, for service to God, and MT members function as a model in this regard. Such holiness is evident in the choices a MT member makes in his/her use of time, participation in worship services and evangelistic efforts, as well as other actions that encourage believers to seek God's will and obey.

20. **"Self-controlled"** (Titus)
In all things, MT members are to maintain a God-honoring personal discipline in public and private, being careful to consider their motives before offering their thought or choosing a particular course of action. They keep a tight rein on their emotions and their tongues, so as not to exacerbate problems or inflame emotionally-charged situations. This frees them to focus on what the Holy Spirit is seeking to communicate in a given situation. It also allows them to act as a model for other Church members.

Other Requirements

Beyond these biblical requirements, the members of the MT of MPFBC believe that our Lord Jesus Christ, and every member of this Church, may expect each member of the MT to serve as a model in the following areas by:

- Attending all Church services unless otherwise hindered by a reason that is approved in good conscience.
- Being a faithful and systematic tither, knowing that the tithe is the minimum requirement that should be brought to the local storehouse (church) for the Lord's work.
- Being evangelistic and missionary in spirit, deeply interested in the salvation of people at home and abroad (see Acts 8).
- Being fully cooperative with the Senior Pastor, PLT, and the Church.
- Being able to refrain from destructive criticism, willing to settle all differences in a quiet and Christian manner.
- Keeping in secrecy those things that should not be discussed with others, especially sensitive proceedings from all meetings of the MT.
- Striving for unity among members of the MT. For example, once a decision has been made at a team meeting, regardless of how much internal debate and discussion transpire, they should emerge in one accord.
- Being a model of spiritual leadership by setting the standard for interaction and fellowship with others by greeting people in the lobby and worship center before and after each service. They should be especially sensitive to introduce themselves to visitors and those members with whom they are unfamiliar.

(PS) P:\Share\XP\bills book\MT Handbook 1-4-07.wpd

NOMINATING COMMITTEE HANDBOOK

5485 Five Forks Trickum Road
Stone Mountain, GA 30087-3045
Phone: 770.921.1452
www.mpfbc.org

Our vision is to develop people into fully devoted followers of Jesus Christ

Table of Contents

Mountain Park First Baptist Church

5485 FIVE FORKS TRICKUM ROAD • STONE MOUNTAIN, GA 30087
770-921-1452 • FAX 770-564-9526
Web Site www.mpfbc.org

DR. BILL BLANCHARD, SENIOR PASTOR

Dear Nominee,

Any church rises or falls on its leadership. If capable, selfless, committed people are in leadership, a church will be blessed and prosper. If positions are filled with those who are willing but not capable nor committed, a church will struggle and achieve little.

There is a sense in which the direction and success of this Church rests with the Nominating Committee more than any other entity. Why is this so? The nominees for the major leadership positions of our Church are selected, evaluated, and interviewed by this one committee. If their choices are incorrect, the church will suffer. If their choices are good, the church will be blessed.

You are being asked by the Management Team to consider service on the Nominating Committee. Please read the following material to see if you have an interest to serve in this area, and then see if you meet the qualifications. After giving you time to prayerfully consider this service, you will be contacted by a member of the Management Team for an answer. If you feel this could be an area of ministry for you, a time will be scheduled for a visit in your home to discuss this further.

Sincerely,

The Senior Pastor and
The Management Team

2

Composition, Qualifications, and Responsibilities

Composition

The Nominating Committee is composed of the Senior Pastor, Chairman of the Management Team, and nine members of the Church at-large. The Executive Pastor is the PLT representative for the committee.

Qualifications

Members of the Nominating Committee shall be exemplary in their conduct, discreet in judgment, of honest report, full of faith, and conscious that they shall set worthy examples of cooperation, love and loyalty for all members of the Church. They should be faithful at all Sunday services, unless hindered by reason of good conscience, so they are aware of the faithfulness of those they consider for positions. They must also be able to keep in secrecy those things discussed about members as they are considered and evaluated for leadership.

Responsibilities

It is the responsibility of the Nominating Committee to present a slate of nominees at the annual Church conference in October for the Management Team, the Equipping Ministry Team, and the Deacon Ministry Team.

- **Management Team-** The Management Team is the Board of Directors of the Church. It is composed of twelve members of the Church. They provide accountability for the Senior Pastor, ensure the financial integrity of the Church, develop and adopt policies relating to the operation of the Church, supervise personnel matters of the Church, and, as the Board of Directors, handle all corporate affairs and business matters involving the Church. These responsibilities are administered through the Finance subcommittee, Policy and Legal Issues subcommittee, and Personnel subcommittee, each comprised of approximately one-third (⅓) of the Management Team members.

□ **Equipping Ministry Team-** The Equipping Ministry Team is made up of nine members of the Church. It is their task to identify, recruit, equip, lead, and deploy others to be involved in various ministries of the Church, with no time placed on their involvement.

□ **Deacon Ministry Team-** The Deacon Ministry Team (DMT) consists of male members of the Church. The number of nominees needed annually to function effectively in its various ministries shall be determined by the DMT. The DMT serves the Church through pastoral support, Church ordinance administration, benevolence ministry, conflict resolution, and other ministries that are consistent with the DMT calling.

Time Line of Responsibilities

Nominees for the Nominating Committee are elected in October at the annual Church Conference. The Chairman of the Nominating Committee is appointed by the Management Team. An orientation meeting is held for the committee in early November.

The Nominating Committee begins the **selection phase** of its work in early February by asking Church members to recommend names for service on the Management Team, Equipping Ministry Team, and the Deacon Ministry Team. After sufficient time has been given for the Church to recommend names, the Nominating Committee submits additional names and begins evaluations.

After nominees have been chosen and ranked, the **contact phase** begins in early March. When a list of nominees is decided upon for each ministry team, the Nominating Committee will contact the nominees to see if they will consider service on the team for which they are nominated. If the answer is affirmative, the appropriate team handbook is mailed to them and a date is set for a personal visit. During the visit, the qualifications and responsibilities of the team to which they are nominated will be discussed and any questions answered.

If the nominee meets the qualifications and accepts the nomination, the **information gathering phase** begins. To make sure the membership knows for whom they are voting at the annual Church conference, a brochure providing information about every nominee on each team is distributed. The Church Bylaws require this to be made available at least two weeks prior to elections at the annual Church conference in October.

To prepare this brochure, each nominee is asked to submit a brief bio and Christian testimony, and have their photo taken. When everything is turned in for each nominee, the work of the Nominating Committee is completed for that year. Normally, this should be done by late May.

Other Requirements

Beyond these biblical requirements, the members of the Nominating Committee of MPFBC believe that our Lord Jesus Christ, and every member of this Church, may expect each member of the Nominating Committee to serve as a model in the following areas by:

- Being a faithful and systematic tither, knowing that the tithe is the minimum requirement that should be brought to the local storehouse (church) for the Lord's work.
- Being evangelistic and missionary in spirit, deeply interested in the salvation of people at home and abroad (see Acts 8).
- Being fully cooperative with the Senior Pastor, PLT, and the Church.
- Being able to refrain from destructive criticism, willing to settle all differences in a quiet and Christian manner.
- Striving for unity among members of the Nominating Committee. For example, once a decision has been made at a meeting, regardless of how much internal debate and discussion transpire, they should emerge in one accord.
- Being a model of spiritual leadership by setting the standard for interaction and fellowship with others by greeting people in the lobby and worship center before and after each service. They should be especially sensitive to introduce themselves to visitors and those members with whom they are unfamiliar.

(ps) P:\Share\XP\bills book\NomCom Handbook 1-29-07.wpd

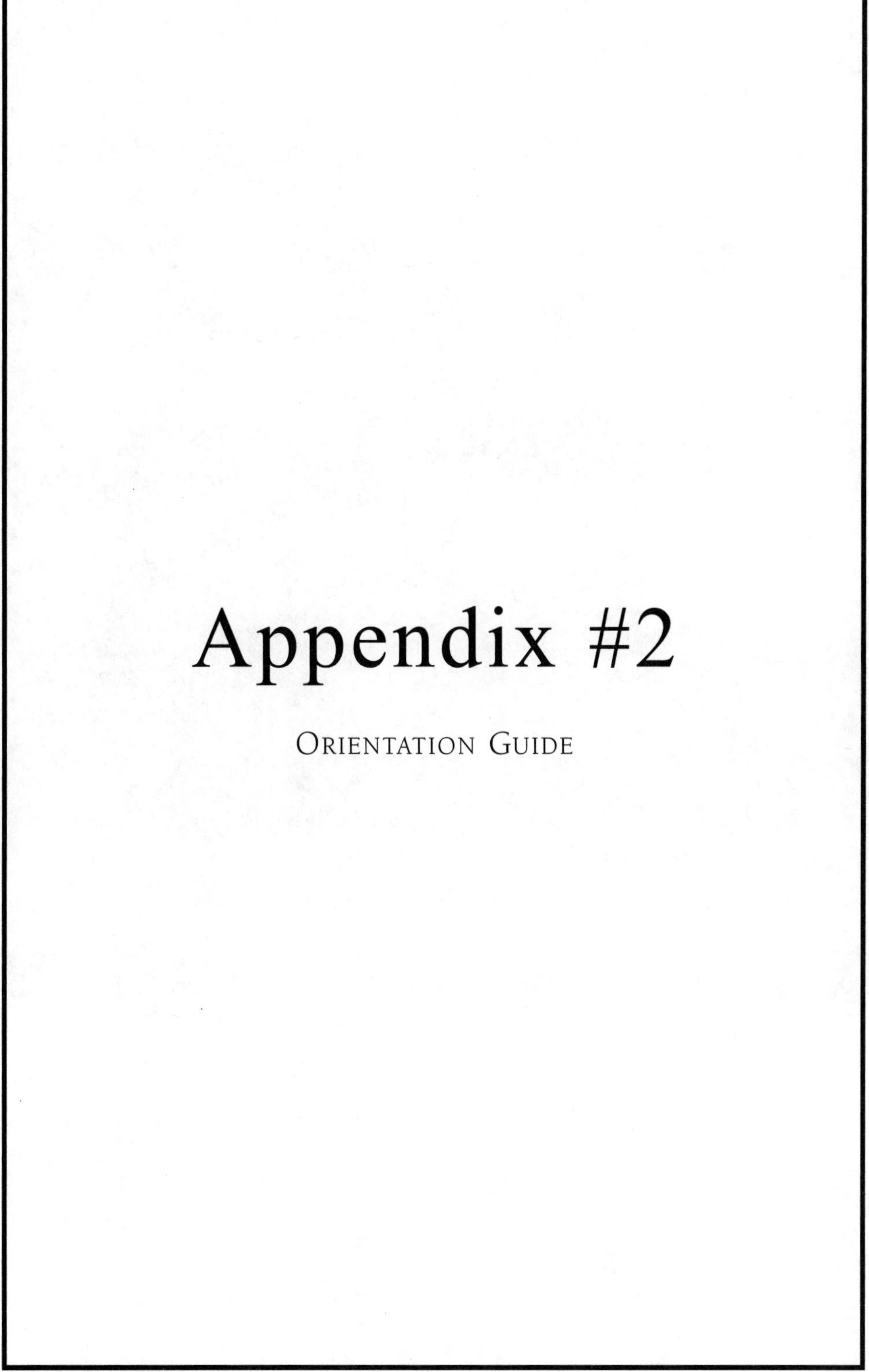

Appendix #2

Orientation Guide

CHURCH STRUCTURE: An Effective Biblical Model

Orientation Guide for Members of the:

- ◆ Nominating Committee
- ◆ Deacon Ministry Team
- ◆ Equipping Ministry Team
- ◆ Management Team

Your Role in Lay Leadership

MOUNTAIN PARK FIRST BAPTIST CHURCH
5485 Five Forks Trickum Road ◆ Stone Mountain, GA 30087
770.921.1452 ◆ www.mpfbc.org
Dr. Bill Blanchard, Senior Pastor

Our vision is to develop people into fully devoted followers of Jesus Christ.

Empowered by prayer, we seek to accomplish our Vision by focusing upon the five eternal purposes of the church whereby we proclaim, through word and deed, the Gospel of the Lord Jesus Christ through:

1) **WORSHIP/MAGNIFICATION**
Because Jesus Christ is the Head of The Church, His Body, He is to have preeminence in all things.

2) **EVANGELISM/MISSIONS**
As Jesus Christ is exalted in worship, His life is extended through His people (personally and corporately) in missionary activity to reach the lost of this world as His mission becomes our mission. Both evangelism and missions are concerned with communicating the good News of Jesus Christ to unbelievers of all cultures.

3) **FELLOWSHIP/MEMBERSHIP**
In an effort to "preserve the unity of the Spirit in the bond of peace" (Ephesians 4:3), God's people will nourish biblically based relationships to create harmony within His Family.

4) **DISCIPLESHIP/MATURITY**
God's people must be equipped to live the Christ-life and then extend His life to others in such a manner that spiritual reproduction occurs for each succeeding generation.

5) **SERVICE/MINISTRY**
As God's people grow in spiritual maturity, they are encouraged to model a ministry lifestyle which will be determined primarily by their God-given SHAPE (Spiritual giftedness, Heart, Abilities, Personality, and Experiences).

We are to be Christian instruments of God who care for the needs of the whole person by stressing a balanced perspective among each of these purposes concurrently. As such, our mission is to magnify God (Worship), while bringing people to the Lord Jesus Christ (Evangelism/Missions) and membership into His Family (Fellowship), growing them in spiritual maturity (Discipleship), and equipping them for service (Ministry).

1

Dear Lay Ministry Leader:

As you prepare to enter into a period of service on your respective committee or team, it is important that you see your role in a proper biblical perspective.

This booklet briefly outlines the four major lay leadership groups in our church: the Nominating Committee, the Deacon Ministry Team, the Equipping Ministry Team and the Management Team. You will also be receiving more specific information about the lay ministry group for which you have been chosen. Although each group has different functions and duties, each group is interrelated. Consider this passage in I Peter 5:1-5:

> *The* ***elders*** *who are among you I exhort, I who am a fellow elder and a witness of the sufferings of Christ, and also a partaker of the glory that will be revealed;* ***shepherd*** *the flock of God which is among you, serving as* ***overseers****, not by compulsion but willingly, not for dishonest gain but eagerly; nor as being lords over those entrusted to you, but being examples to the flock; and when the Chief Shepherd appears, you will receive the crown of glory that does not fade away.*
>
> *Likewise you younger people, submit yourselves to your* ***elders****. Yes, all of you be submissive to one another and be clothed with humility for God resists the proud, but gives grace to the humble.*

The terms found in this passage in I Peter 5 are found throughout the New Testament. All three words in bold print in that passage refer to the same church office:

1. Elders. This word can also be translated "presbyters," and from it we get Presbyterian. It is a transliteration of the Greek word πρεσβύτερος (*presbuteros*). Elder does not necessarily refer to a person's age, although age and experience can apply. But primarily the term elder applies to one's **spiritual maturity**. For example, Timothy was the elder of the church in Ephesus, but he was actually a very young man in chronological years. So the primary meaning of "elder" here should relate to **spiritual maturity** rather than age.

2. Shepherd/Pastor comes from the Greek verb ποιμαίνω (*pōimainō*), which means to provide **pastoral care** by feeding and nourishing.

3. Overseers comes from ἐπισκοπος (*episkopos*), which is defined as a church leader who oversees the **management and governance** of the church. The actual word in this passage, ἐπισκοποῦντες, means "to take the oversight of." From *episkopos* we get "Episcopalian," and that particular denomination calls its leaders "bishops," a word which is seen in other translations of the Bible.

QUESTION: What is the difference between:

Remember that in this passage, all three Greek words (*presbuteros, pōimainō, episkopos*) are addressed to the *same* church leaders. What Peter is saying, paraphrased, is "to the elders/presbyters, be shepherds/pastors as you lead/manage/govern/offer direction as overseers/bishops."

If you go to Acts 20, verses 17 and 28, you will find the same thing: the "***elders** of the church" are to serve as "**overseers**" over "all the flock ... to **shepherd** the church of God which He purchased with His own blood.*"

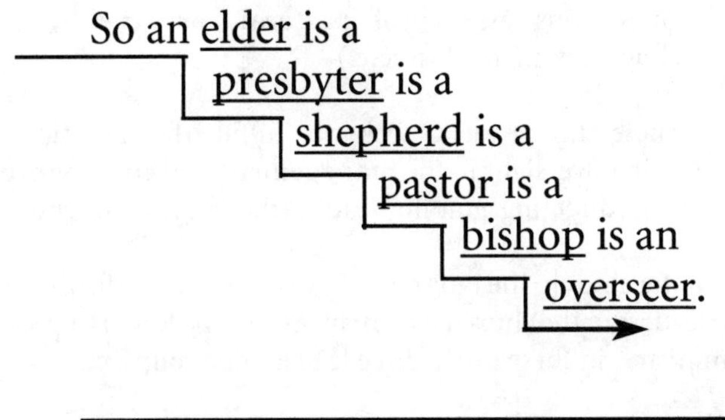

WHAT'S THE POINT OF ALL THIS WORD STUDY?

It really doesn't matter what you call this individual. These titles simply refer to **three different tasks expected of the same person or church office**.

God has called some to the full-time gospel ministry. In our church we call these vocational servant leaders our Pastoral Leadership Team (PLT), and they are called to serve in accordance with the passage in I Peter 5 to function as elders/presbyters, shepherds/pastors, and bishops/overseers.

In addition to fulfilling these functions themselves, the members of our PLT are also to equip three different lay leadership groups within our church in each of these areas. These three groups are:

1. Equipping Ministry Team. This group of lay leaders seeks to fulfill the function of elders/presbyters as they assist others to develop their **spiritual maturity**. How? Through involvement in various church ministry teams according to the SHAPE (Spiritual gifts, Heart, Abilities, Personality, Experiences) God has given them.

2. Deacon Ministry Team. This lay leadership group seeks to fulfill the function of pastors/shepherds through various aspects of **pastoral care** (i.e. feeding, nourishing, caring, counseling, seeking the lost, etc.)

3. Management Team. These lay leaders seek to fulfill the function of overseers/bishops by exercising oversight in the **management and governance** of the church (i.e. administrating, directing, guiding, leading the affairs of the church).

A fourth leadership group in the church, the Nominating Committee, performs a key role in identifying those lay leaders in the church who may possess the leadership skills, as well as the SHAPE for ministry, in these other three leadership groups.

All four groups together, with the assistance and leadership of the Pastoral Leadership Team, serve to fulfill the exhortation found in I Peter 5 and in Acts 20.

Whatever your role may be in ministry, it is helpful to understand how all leadership functions fit together as a unified whole—not competitively, but cooperatively, in developing people into fully devoted followers of Jesus Christ by following God's five, eternal purposes for His Church.

May God bless you richly as you work for Him.

Devotedly your pastor,

Bill Blanchard, Senior Pastor
Mountain Park First Baptist Church

FUNCTIONAL CHART

MOUNTAIN PARK FIRST BAPTIST CHURCH
5485 Five Forks Trickum Road ◆ Stone Mountain, GA 30087

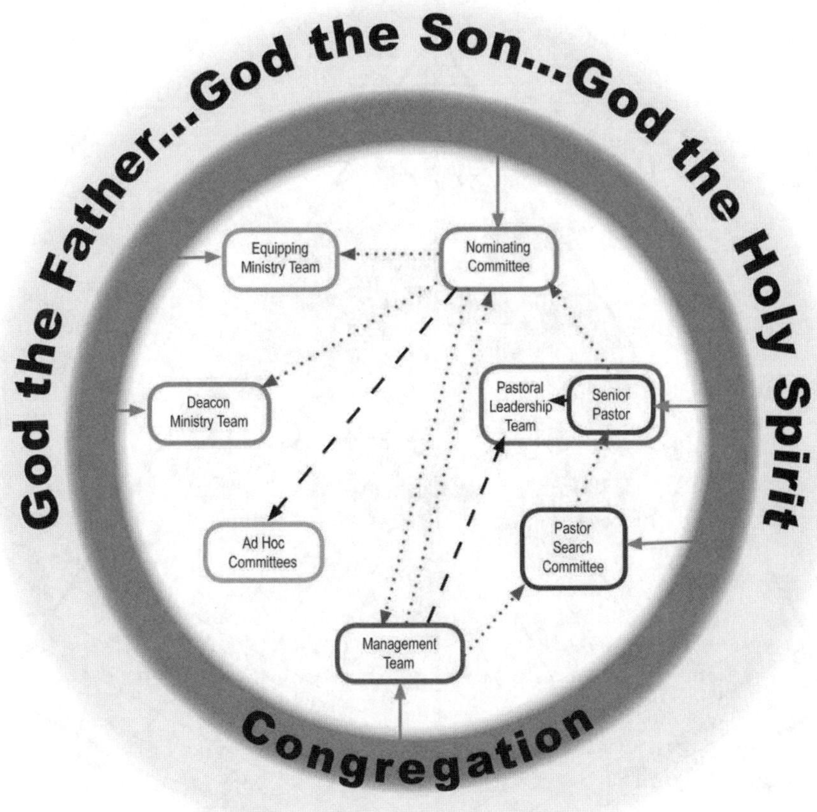

FLOW CHART

MOUNTAIN PARK FIRST BAPTIST CHURCH
5485 Five Forks Trickum Road ◆ Stone Mountain, GA 30087

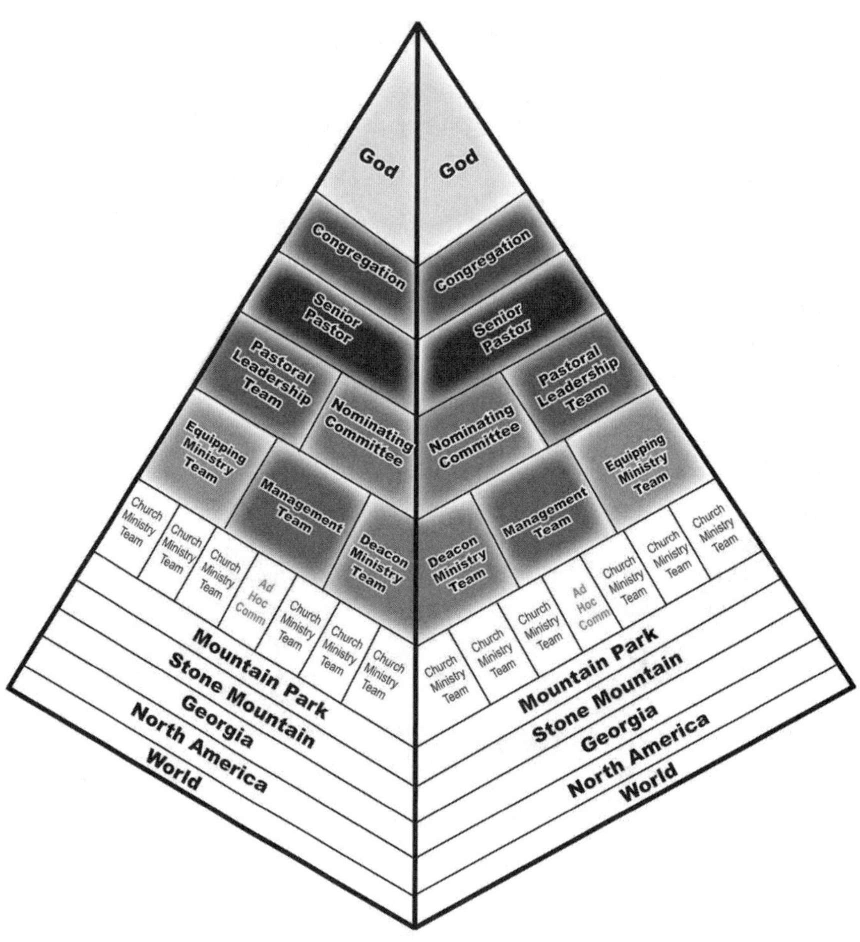

Appendix #3

SHAPE Document

Your SHAPE Personal Profile

God made each of us a part of His spiritual body, the Church. The work God is doing on earth to complete His will is like a big puzzle. Each member of our church is a part of that ministry puzzle. We fit into God's plan according to the shape He has given us. The Pastoral Leadership Team and the Equipping Ministry Team of the Mountain Park First Baptist Church have created a questionnaire using the acronym "shape" to help you determine your SHAPE for ministry in God's Kingdom.

SHAPE stands for
- **S**piritual Gifts
- **H**eart
- **A**bilities
- **P**ersonality
- **E**xperiences

The Equipping Ministry Team asks that you please take time to complete the following member survey. Please return it to the church office or to a member of the Equipping Ministry Team. A member of our Equipping Ministry Team can then contact you and assist you further in finding your place of ministry at Mountain Park First Baptist Church.

Personal Information (Please Print)

Name ______________________________ Date of Birth: ____/____/____

Mailing Address ____

City __________________________ State __________ Zip ___________

Phones: Home (_____)__________ Work (_____)__________

Fax: (_____)__________ Home E-mail address: ______________________

Work E-mail address: ______________________

I joined MPFBC by:
- ☐ Profession of faith and/or baptism
- ☐ Statement of faith
- ☐ Transfer of church membership

Check the following that apply:
- ☐ I'm a licensed/ordained minister
- ☐ I'm an ordained deacon
- ☐ I'm commissioned as a missionary

☐ I am a member of Sunday School only

Mountain Park First Baptist Church
5485 Five Forks Trickum Road
Stone Mountain, GA 30087-3045
770.921.1452
Dr. Bill Blanchard, Senior Pastor
Developing People Into Fully Devoted Followers of Jesus Christ

Spiritual Gifts Inventory

The Bible lists spiritual gifts in a few key passages in the New Testament. You should take time to familiarize yourself with such passages as Romans 12:6-8 and I Corinthians 12:4-12, 27-31. Although not all spiritual gifts are included in the following inventory, the ones listed are the most utilized within our local congregation. After reading a brief description of the following gifts, on a scale of 1-10 (10 being the greatest), mark how this description applies to you. Put the appropriate number (1-10) on the line to the left.

Examples of How to Chart Your Giftedness:
1 (doesn't apply) 3 (applies slightly) 5 (average) 7 (quite a bit) 10 (very much so)

_____ **Prophecy** – Possess strong communication skills; feel God's leadership and power when speaking; direct or to the point in conversations; offers advice that is insightful; aims at the heart of problems and not prone to beat around the bush; interested in what is true, not others' opinions; seems always able to look at a situation and pinpoint the exact problem or cause and a solution.

_____ **Service** – Aware of others' needs and concerns; desires to be helpful in specific and practical ways; warm, caring and loving; levelheaded in crisis situations; works in the background as a support person to the visible leadership; seems incapable of saying "no" when his or her help is needed or asked for; may work to help others, even when he must neglect himself.

_____ **Teaching** – Desire to speak truth in ways that nurture growth and encouragement; explain difficult ideas in a way that people can easily understand; can analyze, explain and interpret facts; even when talking, tend to have a "teachy" style; have ability to focus attention on problems and issues to solve them scripturally; willingness to "be an example" to others in your life.

_____ **Exhortation** – Has an ability to give stirring and inspiring talks or advice; sensitive to others' problems and dilemmas; though you are usually very understanding of people's weaknesses, you can be direct at times–but without being offensive or intimidating; tend to be more of a coach than a drill sergeant; others feel encouraged after spending time with him or her.

_____ **Giving** – Though quality is important, he has an appreciation for simple, natural pleasures; is willing to share material possessions with others; look to meet the needs of others without being asked; care deeply for others and will personally do without to help a cause; deep sense of satisfaction in sharing your own personal resources with others privately or anonymously.

_____ **Administration** – Interested in organization and helping others accomplish tasks; confident standing before others and answering for your work; possess the abilities to see needs and plan how to meet those needs; hardworking; give attention to detail and to tedious items that take patience; concerned about taking the proper steps to complete a job; good at managing your personal time.

_____ **Mercy** – Very caring toward others; bears others' burdens as if they were his own; senses others' hurts, needs, pain and grief; always ready to help those who are weak, frail or disadvantaged; a deep sense of inner joy for doing deeds of goodness to others; even when others have let you down, you tend to be gracious and forgiving very quickly.

_____ **Evangelism** – Naturally enjoy talking to people about your faith; the idea of inviting people to Christ is more of a challenge than a fear; faithful to follow God's will despite personal longings or desires; comfortable with all different kinds of people; enjoy communicating with others and can disarm peoples' fears easily; sensitive to the Holy Spirit when speaking to others about Christ.

_____ **Prayer** – Able to put into words what you heart is feeling; deep inner sense of communion with the Lord; desire to talk to the Lord about all of life's issues; think of devotional life as a secret place of intimacy to be protected; willing to share your innermost spiritual needs only with those whom you trust; tend to take personal needs to God instead of ignoring them or asking others for help.

_____ **Hospitality** – Outgoing; informal; friendly; welcoming to friends and strangers; able to make others feel comfortable, even in unfavorable circumstances; desire to do things for others joyfully; desire to do simple acts of kindness without repayment; sensitive to help others without being asked; will endure being inconvenienced so others can enjoy comfort and convenience; you find deep joy in entertaining others.

Go back to determine your top three gifts, based on the scores, and list them below:

1. ______________________________ Score (1-10) ________

2. ______________________________ Score (1-10) ________

3. ______________________________ Score (1-10) ________

Heart

In this section of our inventory, we want to find out your burdens and things about which you feel passionately. We believe if you have little love for where you serve the Lord, then you won't have a great sense of personal fulfillment. It is possible that in the past you were placed in a position for which you had no concern or love. With this inventory of your SHAPE, we hope that will never happen again. Please continue below and identify your areas of interest so we can help you serve God in a place that matches who He made you to be. In which of the following areas are you more personally concerned and self-confident? Please check all that apply.

People
- ☐ Infants/Toddlers
- ☐ Children
- ☐ Students
- ☐ Singles/College
- ☐ Singles/Career
- ☐ Singles/Adult
- ☐ Single Parents
- ☐ Young Adults
- ☐ Middle Adults
- ☐ Seniors
- ☐ People Far from God
- ☐ Special Needs Children
- ☐ Divorced
- ☐ Abused
- ☐ Mentally Handicapped
- ☐ Internationals
- ☐ Homeless
- ☐ Unemployed

Issues/Ministry
- ☐ Men's Issues
- ☐ Women's Issues
- ☐ Singles' Issues
- ☐ Family/Parenting
- ☐ Marital Issues
- ☐ Ministry/Service
- ☐ Student Issues
- ☐ Environmental Issues
- ☐ School/Educational Matters
- ☐ Politics/Legal Matters
- ☐ Social/Ethical/Moral Issues
- ☐ Ethnic/Racial Concerns
- ☐ Inner-City Missions
- ☐ Missions Education
- ☐ Disaster Relief
- ☐ Other ______________
- ☐ Other ______________
- ☐ Other ______________
- ☐ Other ______________

General Areas
- ☐ Evangelism
- ☐ Discipleship
- ☐ Fellowship
- ☐ Prayer Ministry
- ☐ Teaching
- ☐ Music/Worship
- ☐ Church Worker Training
- ☐ Local Missions
- ☐ State Missions
- ☐ National Missions
- ☐ International Missions
- ☐ Administration
- ☐ Communication/Publicity
- ☐ The Arts
- ☐ Other ______________
- ☐ Other ______________
- ☐ Other ______________
- ☐ Other ______________
- ☐ Other ______________

Pastoral Care
- ☐ Disabled
- ☐ Hearing Impaired
- ☐ Nursing Home Visitation
- ☐ Shut-Ins
- ☐ Assisted Living
- ☐ Widow(ers)/Bereaved
- ☐ Sick/Hospital Visitation
- ☐ Grief Counseling
- ☐ Divorce Recovery
- ☐ Altar Workers
- ☐ Prayer Intercessor
- ☐ Home bound Visitation
- ☐ Benevolence

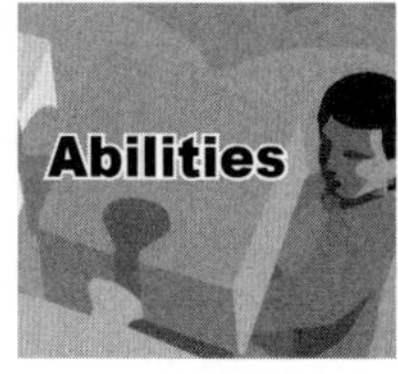

Abilities/Availability

Many times church leaders talk a lot about discovering your spiritual gift, but say very little about the natural abilities which God has given. We believe that abilities and skills should be used in God's service just as spiritual gifts or any other aspect of our person-hood. God gave us both–spiritual gifts and abilities. The only difference is that one was given to us at physical birth or throughout life (our skills and abilities), while the other was given at our re-birth (our spiritual gifts). All of them, however, can be used by God when we are available to Him! Please check the boxes below which indicate special abilities you have used or are now using.

Specific Church Ministries

- ☐ Benevolence
- ☐ Christian Life & Ethics
- ☐ Fellowship
- ☐ Greeter
- ☐ Host/Hostess
- ☐ Library
- ☐ Missions
- ☐ Stewardship
- ☐ Bible Study Leadership
- ☐ Usher
- ☐ Student Ministry
- ☐ FMC Volunteer
- ☐ Bus Driver
- ☐ Van Driver
- ☐ Other ______________

Administration

- ☐ Insurance Evaluation
- ☐ Accounting/Bookkeeping
- ☐ Computers/Programming
- ☐ Constitution/Bylaws
- ☐ Familiarity with Software
- ☐ Media/Library
- ☐ Legal Counsel
- ☐ Financial Planning
- ☐ Parliamentary Procedure
- ☐ Secretarial
- ☐ Treasurer/Trustee
- ☐ Office Volunteer
- ☐ Power Point Experience
- ☐ Excel Experience
- ☐ Other ______________
- ☐ Other ______________

Building/Maintenance

- ☐ Painting
- ☐ Landscaping
- ☐ Construction
- ☐ Maintenance
- ☐ Electrical
- ☐ Plumbing
- ☐ Heating & Air
- ☐ Purchasing
- ☐ Roofing
- ☐ Janitorial
- ☐ Vehicle Maintenance
- ☐ Other ______________
- ☐ Other ______________

Preschool/Children

- ☐ Sunday School
- ☐ Extended Session
- ☐ Kid Zone Music
- ☐ Kid Zone Missions
- ☐ Music Camp
- ☐ Worship for Children
- ☐ Worship for Preschool
- ☐ Vacation Bible School
- ☐ Church Camp
- ☐ Other ______________
- ☐ Other ______________

Recreation

- ☐ Sports ______________
- ☐ Camping ____________
- ☐ Skiing–Snow
- ☐ Skiing–Water
- ☐ Hiking/Climbing
- ☐ Canoeing/Rafting
- ☐ Coaching ___________
- ☐ Aerobics
- ☐ Biking–Mountain
- ☐ Biking–Tour
- ☐ Golf
- ☐ Ropes Course
- ☐ Personal Trainer
- ☐ First-Aid
- ☐ CPR
- ☐ Tennis
- ☐ Gardening/Horticulture
- ☐ Other ______________
- ☐ Other ______________

Music/The Arts

- ☐ Sound Technician
- ☐ Sound Engineer
- ☐ Video Technician
- ☐ Guitar ______________
- ☐ Orchestra Instrument: ______________
- ☐ Choir–Adult
- ☐ Choir–Student
- ☐ Choir–Children
- ☐ Choir–Senior Adult
- ☐ Vocal Soloist
- ☐ Instrumental Soloist
- ☐ Sewing/Costuming
- ☐ Arts & Crafts
- ☐ Acting/Drama/Reading
- ☐ Conducting/Directing
- ☐ Mime/Clowning
- ☐ Keyboards–Piano
- ☐ Keyboards–Organ
- ☐ Composer/Arranger
- ☐ Painting
- ☐ Photography
- ☐ Design
- ☐ Lighting
- ☐ Music/Video Editing
- ☐ Digital Artist
- ☐ Software Designer
- ☐ Decorating

Other

- ☐ Medical Background ______________
- ☐ Dental Background ______________
- ☐ Travel Planning/Agent
- ☐ Hospitality
- ☐ Decorating/Arrangement
- ☐ Transportation
- ☐ Commercial Drivers License
- ☐ Public Speaking
- ☐ Scout Liaison
- ☐ Moderating Meetings
- ☐ Foreign Language: ______________
- ☐ Counselling
- ☐ Cooking/Food Preparation
- ☐ Catering
- ☐ Chaperone–Youth
- ☐ Chaperone–Children
- ☐ Other ______________

- ☐ I am willing to open my home/property occasionally for studies or socials.
- ☐ I have property/home on the lake/mountains/beach that may be used for church retreats for small groups.
- ☐ I have a swimming pool and will host pool parties.

Availability (this helps us see when your schedule is most open to serve the Lord)

- ☐ I am available–call whenever help is needed
- ☐ I am occasionally free to serve during weekday mornings
- ☐ I am occasionally free to serve during weekday afternoons
- ☐ I am occasionally free to serve on weeknights
- ☐ I am sometimes available to serve on Saturday mornings
- ☐ I am sometimes available to serve on Saturday afternoons
- ☐ I am sometimes available to serve on Sunday afternoons
- ☐ I am generally free to serve during the summer (weekdays)
- ☐ I am available to serve more in the school year than other times of the year
- ☐ I am available during Sunday morning services
- ☐ I am available during Sunday evening services
- ☐ I am available during Wednesday activities

Personality

We each have a different personality that influences everything about us. Out personalities help define who we are. Our ministry areas inside and outside the church need a mixture of temperaments and perspectives, which is why we invite you to complete the personality inventory below. We want to find the perfect fit for your unique SHAPE Read the following descriptions of the four basic personality types. Then evaluate your own personality based on those descriptions and rank them, from 1-4 (with 4 being the most like you, 3 being the second most like you, and so on), in the order of how well you match each of them.

_____ **Lion (Choleric)** – Naturally outgoing, assertive, businesslike; at ease with large groups, confident, direct, decisive, success-oriented, optimistic. Dislikes slow decision making and incompetence; strong-willed, not overly dependent on others; wants to be the best, natural leader; deals well with pressure and stress; presses hard to reach goals; is bold during times of adversity and hardship; risk-taker, influential.

_____ **Otter (Sanguine)** – Bubbly and enthusiastic; fashionable, at ease with groups; expressive, spontaneous, deep desire to be popular or liked; excitable, is persuasive and motivational; dislikes monotonous routines and rigid rules; upbeat and positive; initiates fun, tells great stories, makes decisions and asks questions later; humorous, charming, wants others' happiness above all else; independent, good at improvising and "shooting from the hip."

_____ **Golden Retriever (Phlegmatic)** – Loyal and gentle, likes to be comfortable and practical; low key, good listener, sensitive to others' needs; tolerant of others' mistakes, easygoing, relationships are a high priority; peaceful attitude, good peacekeeper between those at odds; dislikes abruptness, insensitivity and confrontation; doesn't overestimate himself; has a servant's attitude; consistent, team player, strives for group agreement; cooperative, tough negotiator and good at bargaining.

_____ **Beaver (Melancholy)** – Reserved, thorough and thoughtful; often prefers privacy over large groups, systematic; perfection is a priority, dislikes surprises and unexpected situations, fears embarrassment, thinker, meticulous, thorough, devoted, philosophical and well-researched, sticks with what works and has worked; efficient and often organized; is cautious in unfamiliar territory; not overly affected by criticism or popularity issues.

Now, please list your top two personality types below:

1.______________________ 2.______________________

Hang in there, we're almost finished!

5

Experiences

God has given each of us experiences in life. Whether they are pleasant or unfavorable, we are to use them for God's glory and allow Him to maximize our past blessings and redeem our past mistakes. Sometimes, certain jobs we have held, or hobbies and recreational activities, would make us better fit to serve in one area than in another.

What jobs have you held?

- ☐ Legal Profession ________________________
- ☐ Medical Profession ________________________
- ☐ Accounting Profession ________________________
- ☐ Computer Profession ________________________
- ☐ Engineer ________________________
- ☐ Trade ________________________
- ☐ Other ________________________
- ☐ Other ________________________

What types of recreation do you enjoy?

1. ________________________
2. ________________________
3. ________________________

Educational Background – I Attended:

- ☐ Public schools
- ☐ Christian schools
- ☐ College at ________________________
  and majored in ________________________
- ☐ Graduate school at ________________________
  and majored in ________________________
- ☐ Doctorate in ________________________
- ☐ Certified in ________________________

Spiritual Background:

- ☐ I became a Christian as a child
- ☐ I became a Christian as a teenager
- ☐ I became a Christian as an adult
- ☐ I am not sure of my spiritual condition
- ☐ I grew up in a Southern Baptist or other Baptist church
- ☐ I didn't grow up regularly attending church
- ☐ I have received limited one-on-one discipleship
- ☐ I consider myself a new Christian or unfamiliar with much of the Bible
- ☐ Before coming to MPFBC, my denominational background was primarily ________________________
- ☐ Someone personally took me under their wing after becoming a Christian and discipled me
- ☐ I grew up atheist/agnostic
- ☐ I grew up with a religious background in ________________________
- ☐ I attended seminary

Painful Experiences – Each of us has had life experiences that have taught us valuable lessons. Are there experiences that the Lord brought you through which, under the right circumstances, you could use to minister to others experiencing a similar situation? Only if you have the liberty and desire to, please share that with us.

____

____

____

____

Do you have suggestions about how to improve this survey? ________________________

____

Thank you for taking the time to complete this S. H. A. P. E. profile. Please return it to the church office or to a member of the Equipping Ministry Team. A member of our Equipping Ministry Team can then contact you and assist you further in finding your place of ministry here at Mountain Park First Baptist Church.

Appendix #4

SHAPE Database Codes

"SHAPE" DATABASE CODES

Most church management software programs let you add "profile codes" to each member record. These profile codes are "user-defined," which means that you can set them up to indicate whatever you choose. Usually you have a number of code-spaces you can use. Our particular church management software is the Shelby System, so I will illustrate with it.

Our profile codes can be a maximum of six letters or numbers. For instance, we can code all deacons to be "deacon," but that is very limiting. To indicate active/inactive deacons we could use "deaact" or "deaina." To indicate ordained deacons and ministers, we could use "orddea" and "ordmin."

To code the SHAPE document categories, our first letter is either an S, an H, an A, a P or an E. The first category is **S**piritual gifts, so we numbered them as they were listed in the document (refer to SHAPE document, page 2, in appendix #3). The first Spiritual Gift (SG code) is Prophecy and it became coded as "SG1." The second Spiritual Gift to be listed is Service, so it became "SG2."

With the "**H**eart" category, it becomes more involved due to the four categories under "Heart." We used "H" for the "**H**eart" category, "P" for the "**P**eople" subcategory, and then gave the number in which they were listed. For example, a person who indicated that they had a "Heart" for working with college singles was coded "HP4."

As you look at the SHAPE document categories, and then look at the "SHAPE Document Reference Guide" following this page, you will quickly see how we coded every category. Remember, "simpler is better." Try to use as *few* codes as possible and make them meaningful. Also, be sure to keep a list of all the codes you use, preferably in a spreadsheet as we have done. For those who forget where they save things on the computer, get in the habit of putting the full computer path name on the last page of the document. On our example you will see: (PS) [Publications Secretary] U:\Excel\SHAPE document reference codes.xls. Also, when a secretary or ministerial staff person leaves, they do not take with them the knowledge of where particular files are stored. The path immediately lets you know which work station, program, and folder the file is in.

SHAPE Document Reference Guide

"S" codes		"H" codes		"A" codes		"P" codes		"E" codes	
Spiritual Gifts		**Heart**		**Abilities**		**Personality**		**Experiences**	
Prophecy	SG1	**People**		**Specific Chrch Min**		Lion	P1	Jobs	
Service	SG2	Infants / Toddlers	HP1	Benevolence	AS1	Otter	P2	Legal Profession	EJ1
Teaching	SG3	Children	HP2	Christian Life & Ethics	AS2	Golden Retriever	P3	Medical Profession	EJ2
Exhortation	SG4	Students	HP3	Fellowship	AS3	Beaver	P4	Accounting Profession	EJ3
Giving	SG5	Singles/College	HP4	Greeter	AS4	Lion/Otter	P5	Computer Profession	EJ4
Administration	SG6	Singles/Career	HP5	Host/Hostess	AS5	Lion/Goldn Retrver	P6	Engineer	EJ5
Mercy	SG7	Singles/Adult	HP6	Library	AS6	Lion/Beaver	P7	Trade	EJ6
Evangelism	SG8	Single Parents	HP7	Missions	AS7	Otter/Gold Retrver	P8	Other	EJ7 & Higher
Prayer	SG9	Young Adults	HP8	Stewardship	AS8	Otter/Beaver	P9	**Spiritual Background**	
Hospitality	SG10	Middle Adults	HP9	Bible Study Leadership	AS9	Goldn Rtrvr/Beaver	P10	As a Child	ES1
		Seniors	HP10	Usher	AS10			As a Teenager	ES2
		People far from God	HP11	Student Ministry	AS11			As an Adult	ES3
		Special Needs Child	HP12	FMC Volunteer	AS12			Not sure	ES4
		Divorced	HP13	Bus Driver	AS13			Southern Baptist / Other Baptist	ES5
		Abused	HP14	Van Driver	AS14			Not regularly attending	ES6
		Men. Handicapped	HP15	Other	AS15			Have received 1-on1 Discipleship	ES7
		Internationals	HP16	**Administration**				**Spiritual Background**	
		Homeless	HP17	Insurance Evaluation	AA1			New Christian/Unfamiliar w/ Bible	ES8
		Issues / Ministry		Accounting/Bookkeeping	AA2			Denominational Background	ES9
		Mens Issues	HI1	Computers/Programming	AA3			Was discipled by someone	ES10
		Womens Issues	HI2	Constitution/Bylaws	AA4			Grew up Atheist/Agnostic	ES11
		Singles Issues	HI3	Familiarity w/Software	AA5			Grew up religious bkgrnd of ...	ES12
		Family/Parenting	HI4	Media/Library	AA6			Attended Seminary	ES13
		Marital Issues	HI5	Legal Counsel	AA7			**Educational Background**	
		Ministry/Service	HI6	Financial Planning	AA8			Public Schools	EE1
		Student Issues	HI7	Parliamentary Procedure	AA9			Christian Schools	EE2
		Environmental Issues	HI8	Secretarial	AA10			College	EE3
		School/Educa Matters	HI9	Treasurer/Trustee	AA11			Graduate Study	EE4
		Politics/Legal Matters	HI10	Office Volunteer	AA12			Doctorate	EE5
		Social/Ethical/Moral	HI11	Power Point Experience	AA13			Certified in	EE6
		Ethnic/Racial	HI12	Excel Experience	AA14				
		Inner-City Missions	HI13	Other	AA15				
		Issues / Ministry		**Building/Maintenance**					
		Missions Education	HI14	Painting	AB1				
		Disaster Relief	HI15	Landscaping	AB2				
		Other	HI16 & Higher	Construction	AB3				
		General Areas		Maintenance	AB4				
		Evangelism	HG1	Electrical	AB5				
		Discipleship	HG2	Plumbing	AB6				
		Fellowship	HG3	Heating & Air	AB7				
		Prayer Ministry	HG4	Purchasing	AB8				
				Roofing	AB9				

Spiritual Gifts	Heart	Abilities	Personality	Experiences
	(Issues / Ministry)	**(Building/Maintenance)**		
	Teaching HG5	Janitorial AB10		
	Music/Worship HG6	Vehicle Maintenance AB11		
	Church Wkr Training HG7	Other AA12 & Higher		
	Local Missions HG8	**Preschool/Children**		
	State Missions HG9	Sunday School AC1		
	National Missions HG10	Extended Session AC2		
	Intl Missions HG11	KidZone Music AC3		
	Administration HG12	KidZone Missions AC4		
	Communications/Publ HG13	Music Camp AC5		
	Pastoral Care	Worship w/Children AC6		
	Disabled HC1	**Preschool/Children**		
	Hearing Impaired HC2	Worship w/Preschoolers AC7		
	Nursing Home Visit HC3	Vacation Bible School AC8		
	Shut-ins HC4	Church Camp AC9		
	Assisted Living HC5	Other AC10		
	Widow(ers)/Bereav HC6	**Recreation**		
	Sick/Hospital Visit HC7	Sports AR1		
	Grief Counseling HC8	Camping AR2		
	Divorce Recovery HC9	Skiing-Snow AR3		
	Altar Workers HC10	Skiing-Water AR4		
	Prayer Intercessor HC11	Hiking/Climbing AR5		
	Homebound Visit HC12	Canoeing/Rafting AR6		
	Benevolence HC13	Coaching AR7		
	Other HC14	Aerobics AR8		
		Biking-Mountain AR9		
		Biking-Tour AR10		
		Golf AR11		
		Ropes Course AR12		
		Personal Trainer AR13		
		First Aid AR14		
		Recreation		
		CPR AR15		
		Tennis AR16		
		Gardening/Horticulture AR17		
		Other AR18 & Higher		

		Music/The Arts	
		Sound Technician AM1	
		Sound Engineer AM2	
		Video Technician AM3	
		Guitar AM4	
		Orchestra Instrument AM5	
		Choir-Adult AM6	
		Choir-Student AM7	
		Choir-Children AM8	
		Choir-Senior Adult AM9	
		Vocal Soloist AM10	
		Instrumental Soloist AM11	
		Sewing/Costuming AM12	
		Arts & Crafts AM13	
		Acting/Drama AM14	
		Conducting/Directing AM15	
		Mime/Clowning AM16	
		Keyboards-Piano AM17	
		Keyboards-Organ AM18	
		Composer/Arranger AM19	
		Painting AM20	
		Photography AM21	
		Design AM22	
		Lighting AM23	
		Music/Video Editing AM24	
		Digital Artist AM25	
		Software Designer AM26	
		Decorating AM27	
		Other AM28	
		Other	
		MedicalBackground A01	
		Dental Background A02	
		Travel Planning/Agent A03	
		Hospitality A04	
		Decorating/Arrangement A05	
		Transportation A06	
		Commercial Drivers A07	
		Public Speaking A08	
		Scout Liaison A09	
		Running Meetings A010	
		Foreign Language A011	
		Counseling A012	
		Cooking/Food Prep A013	
		Catering A014	

Spiritual Gifts	Heart	Abilities	Personality	Experiences
		(Other)		
		Chaperone-Youth A015		
		Chaperone-Children A016		
		Availability		
		Call when needed AT1		
		Weekday mornings AT2		
		Weekday afternoons AT3		
		Weeknights AT4		
		Saturday mornings AT5		
		Saturday afternoons AT6		
		Sunday afternoons AT7		
		Weekdays - summers AT8		
		More in school year AT9		
		Sunday AM services AT10		
		Sunday PM services AT11		
		Wed. Activities AT12		
		Other AT13		

(PS) U:\Excel\SHAPE document reference codes.xls

Appendix #5

CHURCH MISSION

Adopted in Church Conference on November 16, 2005

- **VISION**
- **PURPOSES**
- **PRINCIPLES**
- **STRATEGY**
- **INDICATORS OF PROGRESS**

VISION STATEMENT

Our Vision Is To Develop People Into Fully Devoted Followers of Jesus Christ

This Vision Statement comes right out of "The Great Commission" (Matthew 28:18-20), where we are told to go into all the world to:

- Preach the Gospel to the ***lost people*** throughout the world, and
- Teach/Edify ***believers*** that they might become disciples of Jesus Christ.

2

PURPOSES

Empowered by prayer, we seek to accomplish our Vision by focusing upon the five eternal purposes of the church whereby we proclaim, through word and deed, the Gospel of the Lord Jesus Christ through:

1) **WORSHIP/MAGNIFICATION**
   Because Jesus Christ is the Head of The Church, His Body, He is to have preeminence in all things.

2) **EVANGELISM/MISSIONS**
   As Jesus Christ is exalted in worship, His life is extended through His people (personally and corporately) in missionary activity to reach the lost of this world as His mission becomes our mission. Both evangelism and missions are concerned with communicating the good News of Jesus Christ to unbelievers of all cultures.

3) **FELLOWSHIP/MEMBERSHIP**
   In an effort to "preserve the unity of the Spirit in the bond of peace" (Ephesians 4:3), God's people will nourish biblically based relationships to create harmony within His Family.

4) **DISCIPLESHIP/MATURITY**
   God's people must be equipped to live the Christ-life and then extend His life to others in such a manner that spiritual reproduction occurs for each succeeding generation.

5) **SERVICE/MINISTRY**
   As God's people grow in spiritual maturity, they are encouraged to model a ministry lifestyle which will be determined primarily by their God-given SHAPE (Spiritual giftedness, Heart, Abilities, Personality, and Experiences).

We are to be Christian instruments of God who care for the needs of the whole person by stressing a balanced perspective among each of these purposes concurrently. As such our mission is to magnify God (Worship), while bringing people to the Lord Jesus Christ (Evangelism/Missions) and membership into His Family (Fellowship), growing them in spiritual maturity (Discipleship), and equipping them for service (Ministry).

3

FOUNDATIONAL PRINCIPLES

We affirm "The Baptist Faith and Message (2000 edition)" as a doctrinal statement of our Christian beliefs. Therefore, while the following foundational principles fall within the parameters of such a confessional statement, they are also considered here because of their importance in helping us fulfill our vision through the five eternal purposes of His church.

1) The Bible, composed of the sixty-six books of the Old and New Testaments, is the inspired word of God and is truth without mixture of error.

2) Every believer has the responsibility of being a witness for Jesus Christ. Therefore, all believers live under the call to reach out to others within their circle of influence and share with them the truth of the Gospel.

3) The needs of a non-Christian differ from those of a believer. For instance, the unchurched person rarely understands Christian terminology and has little or no knowledge of basic Christian principles. Therefore, it is imperative that believers minister to non-Christians with their perspective in mind.

4) Believers must respect the process that leads from unbelief . . . to faith in Christ . . . to Christian maturity. For the unbeliever, the decision to trust in Jesus Christ is usually preceded by a process of examining and evaluating the claims of the Christian faith. After conversion, believers must respect the process that leads to maturity as the new believer develops into a fully devoted disciple.

5) Because every believer is gifted by God to play a vital role in equipping and maturing the body of Christ, we must attempt to mobilize believers by challenging them to accept roles of leadership and service through the discovery, development, and implementation of their spiritual giftedness.

4

SIX-STEP STRATEGY

The intention of this strategy is to show us how the Lord can help us make our vision statement a reality.

STEP ONE: BUILDING A RELATIONSHIP

Bringing the unchurched into a vital relationship with Jesus Christ and the life of the church will only be accomplished when people who love Jesus Christ are convinced that lost people matter to God and then begin to build relationships with unchurched individuals. These relationships, however, should be handled with integrity, meaning that interactions with unbelievers are to be governed by authentic faith and genuine love; unbelievers should never be treated as "projects."

Unchurched people are usually insulated from Christianity. Rarely do they liste to or watch Christian radio and television, their lives are not touched by bumper sticker evangelism, religious mail that arrives to their homes is likely discarded, and they do not have any intention of visiting a church. Therefore, every believer attending the Mountain Park First Baptist Church is strongly challenged to build relationships of integrity with their unchurched friends.

STEP TWO: SHARING A VERBAL WITNESS

After establishing a relationship of integrity with the unchurched, every believer attending the Mountain Park First Baptist Church should begin to anticipate opportunities to share their personal testimony with them, ask God to provide appropriate moments to do so, and then invite them to one of our worship services where they will be challenged in a relevant way to consider the claims of the Lord Jesus Christ.

STEP THREE: PARTICIPATING IN A SMALL GROUP

As rapport is built, and the idea of a personal relationship with Jesus Christ has been advanced to an unchurched individual, the believer then has an opportunity to invite the unbeliever to a small group environment through the Bible study ministry of our church where encouragement and fellowship are also offered.

STEP FOUR: SERVING IN THE CHURCH

When the unbeliever chooses to accept the saving grace of Jesus Christ, is baptized, and joins his/her life with the local family of God, he/she is encouraged to begin participating in a variety of the many areas of our church's life which are designed to support and edify the believer. They are also urged to discover, develop, and use their spiritual giftedness in some form of Christian service within The Body of Christ so that they can experience their spiritual potential as fully devoted disciples of Jesus Christ.

STEP FIVE: STEWARDSHIP

Acknowledging that all we have comes from God, it is important that every believer recognizes stewardship as a form of discipleship and giving a form of worship. Believers also have a responsibility to manage their money in a God-glorifying manner. This includes living within their means, being gracious with their possessions, sharing with those who are in need, and giving generously to the Lord's work, while learning to avoid coveting material goods and unreasonable indebtedness.

STEP SIX: REPEATING THE CYCLE

In this spiritual process of becoming a fully devoted follower of Jesus Christ ("Vision Statement"), each newly developed believer must join others to set this six-step cycle into motion once more as he/she begins to build bridges with the unchurched (Step One) within his/her own sphere of relationships.

5

INDICATORS OF PROGRESS

Out of the Six-Step Strategy comes a necessary question: How do we know if we are really being effective in achieving our Vision? Although it is difficult to measure "the heart change" of people, the intention of the following quantifiable indicators is that they would serve as monitors for the spiritual progress of our congregation as we are challenged to examine:

- ◇ what ambitions true disciples have,
- ◇ how disciples react in relationship to others, and
- ◇ how disciples invest themselves in their passions for Jesus Christ.

- ♦ Evangelism—The number of lives transformed by knowing and receiving God's saving grace by faith in Jesus Christ. The Scriptures teach that this transformation is to be followed by baptism into the church, the universal Body of Christ (I Corinthians 12:13).

- ♦ Membership—The Bible makes it clear that when a person is spiritually transformed he/she is also adopted into a "Family" to function within the Christian Community rather than be isolated. Therefore, each new believer is encouraged to become an active, participating member in local expressions (Hebrews 10:25) of the world-wide Church.

- ♦ Attendance—
  - a) In worship services
  - b) In Bible study and discipleship training events to develop long-term patterns of spiritual growth.
  - c) In the Discovering Life 101-501 Classes to train people to become contagious Christians.

- ♦ Ministry—The number of people who are identifying and exercising their spiritual gifts in various ministries "for the common good" (I Corinthians 12:7) of the local fellowship.

- ♦ Missions—The number of people involved in mission ministries and trips.

- ♦ Financial giving—In response to God's amazing grace, we should be generous investors of our financial resources into the local fellowship so that the work of God can flourish there and around the world. The regular discipline of giving tithes and additional offerings underscores the Lordship of Jesus Christ over our material resources.

(PS) P:\Share\SrPas\Outlines\Connecting Point\Vision Statement.wpd

Appendix #6

ACRONYMS

ACRONYMS

DMT	Deacon Ministry Team
EMT	Equipping Ministry Team
MT	Management Team
NC	Nominating Committee
PLT	Pastoral Leadership Team
SALT & SPICE	Strategic Advanced Leadership Training and Significant Promotion Inspiration Communication Experience
SHAPE	Spiritual Gifts, Heart/Passion, Abilities, Personality, and Experiences